WARINGTON BADE

CANOE TRAVELLING

LOG OF A CRUISE ON THE BALTIC
AND PRACTICAL HINTS
ON BUILDING AND FITTING CANOES

WITH TWENTY-FOUR ILLUSTRATIONS AND THE MAP

Elibron Classics
www.elibron.com

Elibron Classics series.

© 2005 Adamant Media Corporation.

ISBN 1-4021-7186-2 (paperback)
ISBN 1-4021-2772-3 (hardcover)

This Elibron Classics Replica Edition is an unabridged facsimile of the edition published in 1871 by Smith, Elder, and Co., London.

Elibron and Elibron Classics are trademarks of Adamant Media Corporation. All rights reserved.

This book is an accurate reproduction of the original. Any marks, names, colophons, imprints, logos or other symbols or identifiers that appear on or in this book, except for those of Adamant Media Corporation and BookSurge, LLC, are used only for historical reference and accuracy and are not meant to designate origin or imply any sponsorship by or license from any third party.

CANOE TRAVELLING.

CROSSING THE SOUND.

CANOE TRAVELLING:

LOG OF A CRUISE ON THE BALTIC,

AND PRACTICAL HINTS

ON BUILDING AND FITTING CANOES.

BY

WARINGTON BADEN-POWELL.

WITH TWENTY-FOUR ILLUSTRATIONS AND A MAP.

LONDON:
SMITH, ELDER & CO., 15, WATERLOO PLACE.
1871.

[The Right of Translation is reserved.]

PREFACE.

CANOEING, as a mode of aquatic locomotion, has been in practice many thousand years; and there is as much difference between the canoes of different countries as between the men who use them. The single canoes of East India and the islands of the Pacific and Indian Oceans have made little or no progress beyond the canoes of the early Europeans, which, from time to time, are discovered in an embedded state; though the double and outrigged canoes of the former are a shade better.

In Canada, canoeing is one of the regular modes of travelling, and some wonderful feats—both in distance accomplished and dangerous rapids safely cleared—are performed in single canoes built of birch-bark and manned by one, two, or more paddlers.

The Greenlanders use canoes made of sealskin and built with enormous "kink;" in these they make long sea-voyages and fishing expeditions, often in bad weather; but, owing to their being decked all over, the great kink, and the skill of the canoeist, they seldom come to grief—at least, we seldom hear of it.

Modern canoeing on the rivers in England has—with, perhaps, the exception of coracleing—been in pursuit of exercise and pleasure, rather than of fish or commerce. A few light canoes were to be met with, scattered along the banks of the Thames, chiefly at Eton and Oxford, for the last twenty or thirty years; but the earliest publicly recognized summer cruising abroad dates only from 1865, when the *Rob Roy* was paddled and sailed on the continental lakes and rivers.

Since that time, hundreds of canoes have been built, vast improvements made, other long foreign voyages successfully accomplished; the experiences of each, when made known, helping in the general improvement of canoes and their fittings, till, already in these few years, the first travelling canoes bear no comparison with those of the present time.

In canoe travelling there are two distinct pleasures:

PREFACE.

one, the healthful enjoyment of a free and easy life in fine weather and varied scenery; and the other, the more sensational, cracking on under sail, and working her successfully through and over heavy seas; not in the foolhardy sense "courting danger," though this term is often applied to a man without knowing what really *is* danger to him. A cockney on a cab-horse might accuse a huntsman of "courting danger," for merely jumping a fence; and in the same way with canoeing, a man may be starting in his canoe to cross some hilly water; no one can tell by guessing whether these seas will be a danger to him, owing to his want of experience and caution, or a pleasure, owing to his perfect boat and knowledge of how to work her. Yet there are men who do court danger, either that it may seem bold to others, or to enjoy for a short time the excitement of flitting along the brink of eternity.

There are many lovely wild spots on lakes, rivers, and seas, to which no man can get in his yacht: no railway, no horse, not even his own legs, can take him there. In some cases a rowing boat might avail, but in bad weather the heavy seas would render any open boat work dangerous, if not impossible; or if once there, might detain him beyond his time or will: whereas a good cruising canoe, at once his lifeboat, portable yacht, and house, is equally efficient whether the water be deep or shallow, rough or smooth.

Many imagine that canoe travelling must necessarily be a solitary performance: on the contrary, I think the more the merrier and the safer, provided that each man is "skipper of his own boat." To some men there is an intense enjoyment in being alone with their thoughts in a foreign country for months together, the spell only to be broken at intervals by the necessary intercourse with the natives. I have enjoyed many a short solitary cruise, solitary because mine was the only canoe in those parts of the world; but on a long trip I should prefer as many companions as possible, for, even when two are together, every trouble is halved and pleasure doubled. What can be more enjoyable to a lover of yachting and boating, than to form one in a fleet of these miniature yachts on a cruise; a separate interest is felt for each little ship and its doings, it is one continued regatta and picnic; and while I enjoy an unimpaired brain, I will never get the *Nautilus* " under weigh" for a long cruise, under a self-imposed sentence of solitary confinement.

PREFACE.

One of the great recommendations of canoeing as an invigorating national amusement, is its inexpensiveness. The canoe calls for no heavy outlay in fitting out; no crew to eat their heads off; she is easily housed and easily transported to any portion of the globe. The oak travelling canoe, with gear, built by the best Thames builders, costs about a guinea a foot. During our Swedish tour, a period of two months, we each spent 45*l*., staying at the best hotels, and travelling first class when on steamboat or railway; so of course it could be done cheaper.

Details of that tour will be found in the following log, accompanied by some of its sketches.

Those who contemplate canoe building or travelling may be interested in the particulars of various methods of construction and fittings described in Part II.

May, 1871.

CONTENTS.

PART I.

LOG OF A CRUISE ON THE BALTIC.

CHAP.		PAGE
I.	WHITHER?—THE SHIP—RIGGING—GOTHENBURG	1
II.	GOTHA RIVER—SLEEPING IN CANOES—LILLA EDIT—LIVELY LANDLADY	6
III.	FALLS OF TROLLHATTEN—LAKE WENERN—CARLSTAD—A WET RUN	11
IV.	COW "MAKING TRACKS"—NIGHT IN A HUT—"TOUCH AND GO"—IN THE SURF	17
V.	PIKE AND MOSQUITOES—MARIESTAD PRISON—WEST GOTHA CANAL	22
VI.	YACHT CLUB—MOTALA—TOWING CANOES—LAKE ROXEN	27
VII.	INVISIBLE RIVER—NORRKÖPING—DEER-STALKING AT QVARSEBO	32
VIII.	FIRST DAY ON THE BALTIC—A SHOUT IN THE DARK—OXLÖ SUND	38
IX.	ORSBAKEN—THUNDERSTORM—NOCTURNAL VISITORS—CROSS SEAS	43
X.	MUNICIPAL DUTIES AT TROSA—HEAD-WIND AND SEA—BULLOCK-CART	49
XI.	IN FOR THE "LADY'S MONTH"—STICKY WATER—LUNCHEON AFLOAT	55

CHAP.		PAGE
XII.	STOCKHOLM FROM THE MALAR—EXPERIMENTS—OUR SPECIAL ARTIST	61
XIII.	CARLSKRONA HARBOUR—ARRIVAL AT MALMÖ—BATHS	66
XIV.	"DOCTOR OF SWIMMING"—DROWNED RATS—BRASS BAND	70
XV.	TIN HATCH—BOUND FOR COPENHAGEN—A NORTH-WESTER	74
XVI.	CROSSING THE SOUND—SWAN CHASE—SLEEP ON SALTHOLM	78
XVII.	MIRAGE—TICKLISH FOOTING—SEALS—HARBOUR AFTER DARK	82
XVIII.	COPENHAGEN—THORWALDSEN—KIEL HARBOUR—PRUSSIAN FLEET—HAMBURG	87
XIX.	STREAM WORK—ALSTER LAKE—SUNK! BUT ALL HANDS SAVED	91
XX.	"PUT THAT SAIL DOWN"—GREEN LIGHTS—STREET CANALS	95
XXI.	WATER LABYRINTH—CLOSE SHAVE IN A LOCK—THE ELBE AT LAST—"THE BERLIN"—STARTING FOR LONDON—THE THAMES	99

PART II.

PRACTICAL HINTS ON BUILDING AND FITTING CANOES.

XXII.	"NAUTILUS" No. 1—DEFECTS—DIVING—SINKING—NO CABIN	105
XXIII.	"NAUTILUS" No. 2—DIMENSIONS—RIGS—LIFE-BOAT QUALITIES	109
XXIV.	"NAUTILUS" No. 3—DIMENSIONS—BULKHEADS, &c.	113
XXV.	BUILDING—WOOD—WEIGHTS OF WOOD, &c.	117

CONTENTS.

CHAP.		PAGE
XXVI.	Rigs — Lateen, Settee, Chinese — Dipping Lug — Revolving Lug — Standing Lug — Spreet Sail — Sliding-gunter — Sliding-spreet — Dandy — Foresails	121
XXVII.	Fittings — Paddles — Steering — Rudders — Camping-out — Leeboards — Centreboards — Outriggers — Sideboards — Wheels — Cleats — Pumps — Ballast — Sail-making and Rigging — Hatches and Aprons	140
XXVIII.	Navigation — Charts — Compass — Bearings — Soundings — Variation of Compass — Currents — Leeway — Instruments	160
XXIX.	Cooking and Clothing — Stores of Food — Ship's Stores — Useful Articles — Wood Fires — "Rob Roy" Cuisine — Fresh Water on Salt — Canoe Wardrobe — Night-Cloak — Overland Stores and Town Rigs	168

LIST OF ILLUSTRATIONS.

PART I.

		PAGE
Crossing the Sound	*Frontispiece.*	
Map of the "Track"	*Facing*	1
Turned In		7
The "Isis" Running		18
Which Way?		34
Lighthouse on the Baltic		41
Snow-Plough		56
A Clipping Breeze	*Facing*	97

PART II.

"Nautilus" No. 3	*Facing*	113
Lateen and Settee		124
Chinese Rig		125
Standing Lug and Mizen		128
Spreet-rigged Wherry		131
Sliding-Gunter Brass		133
Sliding-Gunter Rig		134
Sliding-Spreet Rig		136
Rudders and Gear		143
Leeboard		147
Sideboard		148
Canoe Wheels		150
Cleats		151
Pump		152
Sail-cutting		155
Compass Cards		162
Coast Line		164

PART I.

LOG OF A CRUISE ON THE BALTIC.

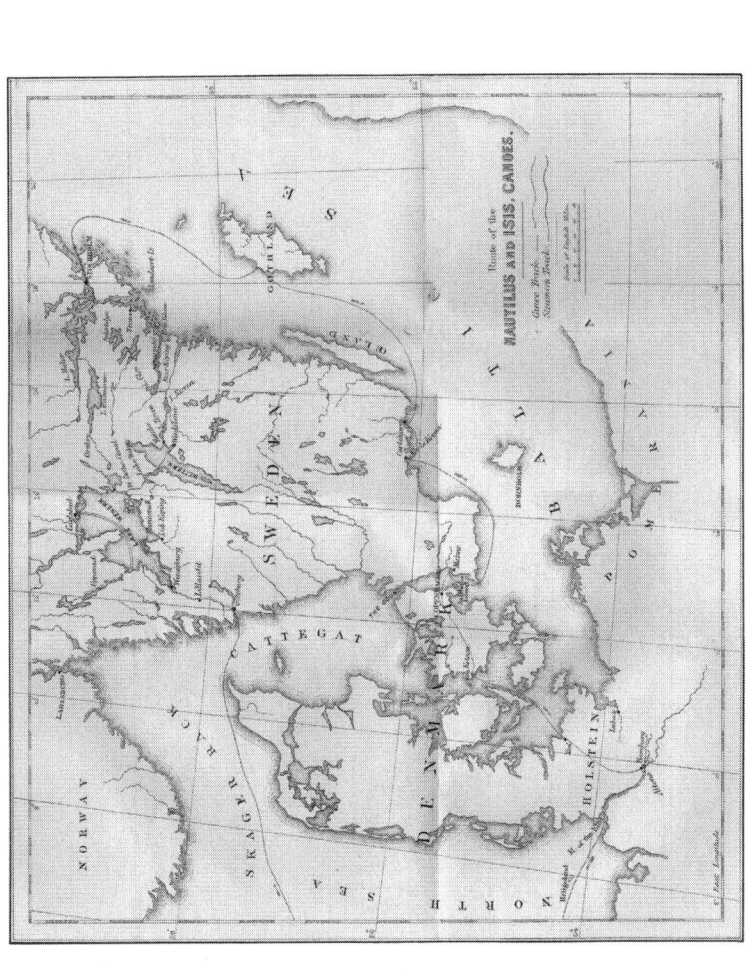

CANOE TRAVELLING.

CHAPTER I.

WHITHER?—THE SHIP—RIGGING—GOTHENBURG.

THE upper portions of the Thames, with a light boat and fine weather, may be satisfactory enough to one man, whilst to another the conditions of recreation will be better fulfilled by roaming through distant countries, with somewhat of danger and difficulty to overcome. A stiff breeze, wild scenery, freedom of dress and action, with the perplexities of a strange language, may be preferred to being guided by a tourists' handbook from a first-class Swiss railway carriage to the comfortable monster hotel, with its obsequious English-speaking waiters.

Freedom of action, a good canoe, and plenty of water, was certainly my idea of the best heading to a chapter on "summer cruising."

CANOE TRAVELLING.

Freedom of action would commence as soon as ever I took my seat in the canoe and shoved off. Next comes the canoe. She was of the *Rob Roy* type, fourteen feet long, two feet two inches beam, and one foot deep from deck to keel, built of oak below, the deck and topstreak being of cedar.

I had found the standing lug rig awkward to handle in sudden squalls; without a mast-traveller, on letting go the halliards, it was apt to bag out to leeward, then bang about in a most disorderly manner, and finally fall into the water; and with a traveller it would often refuse the duty of coming down at all. Of course these little eccentricities could nearly always be "nipped in the bud," but still it was not quite the style of rig for a long cruise.

The sliding-gunter appeared to me the best rig to try, only that it had to be altered in most of its details, so as to adapt it to so small and light a boat. This was accomplished by degrees, till at last a handy, as well as good-looking, rig was fitted to her.

Then the ship's instruments and stores had to be collected and stowed—a compass, aneroid thermometer, charts, lamp, knives, clothes, as well as sleeping, cooking, fishing, carpenter's and artist's gear; stores of preserved soup, tea, coffee, sugar, &c. Boatswain's stores of spare blocks, lines, sails, &c.; carpenter's, of nails, red-lead, varnish, wire, &c. Then followed a two-days' trial, of all the new fittings, on the Thames, and most satisfactorily they performed their various duties.

The difficult question then arose, of "where to go?" One can scarcely tell by merely looking at maps, how far a country may offer really enjoyable water-travelling; for instance, on a map, the banks of the Thames, below London Bridge, *look* just as pleasant as those above Kingston.

Books of European travels are generally confined to the description of towns, roads, and railways; they rarely mention the forest-surrounded lakes and rivers, which form the backbone of a canoe tour.

After due consideration of Europe in general, Sweden appeared to us the most promising water-country. My friend H. and I, therefore, planned to go in our canoes right across Sweden, from Gothenburg on the west coast to Stockholm on the east coast. In round numbers this would give us nearly 300 miles of various lakes, rivers, and bays, besides 50 of the Gotha Canal, and another 50 of the Baltic Sea.* We proposed to go by steamboat from London to Gothenburg, and after some 400 miles of canoeing, to steam home again *viâ* Copenhagen and Hamburg.

The evening of July 17, 1869, closed upon us as we dropped down the Thames, having our canoes, the *Nautilus*

* We did, however, paddle eighty-eight miles on the Baltic.

and the *Isis*, safely slung to the beams on the between-decks of the S.S. *Mary*. With the exception of fouling a brig in Gravesend Reach, the voyage was accomplished without any noteworthy incident, and on the 20th we arrived at Gothenburg, a cheerful-looking thriving town. We paddled along some of its numerous canals, only succeeding after some delay in finding the Gotha Kalary Hotel, for which we had been inquiring, under English pronunciation of its letters, whereas the Swedish pronunciation is Yota Chillery, *g* and *j* before a vowel answering to our *y*; and *k* being generally sounded as *ch* soft.

The town is built chiefly of stone; broad streets at right angles to one another, a canal running down the centre of each, with a wide road and lumpy pavement on either side of it. All heavy traffic goes on the canals, —carriages and light carts only being allowed on the road. There is nothing ancient to be seen; but Gustavus Adolphus judged wisely that such a harbour would soon attract an immense commerce, and great has been the boon to succeeding generations, constantly numerically increasing, who have thriven and prospered on the results of his foresight. Vessels were here from all parts of the world.

Whilst paddling about we came to the swimming-baths, a portion of the harbour being railed off, with dressing-boxes built on the top of the railing. Thus there is a square of dressing-rooms supported two or three feet above the water, the entrance door being on the land side. We looked about to find any way of getting withinside these railings, and spied out one portion whence some bars had been removed to allow the swimmers access to the river. We put the boats through this opening and managed, by bending down, to glide on under the rails, and thus surprised the bathers by the sudden appearance of two canoes in the centre of their swimming-bath.

CHAPTER II.

GOTHA RIVER—SLEEPING IN CANOES—LILLA EDIT—LIVELY LANDLADY.

21*st July.*—AT 5 A.M., after a cup of coffee, our boats were carried down by four men to a canal, and off we paddled, under convoy of a rush of spectators along the banks, men of larger growth as well as such boys as chanced to be already up. Having traversed short portions of canal, we emerged on the fine full-bodied river Gotha, and set sail to a north-westerly breeze. We intended to proceed as far up as the current might permit, and soon found it necessary to take in sail and paddle against a strong head-wind; the wind having shifted.

About 1 P.M. we hauled the canoes ashore on a rocky point, marked on the map as Kattleburg, and quickly had a blazing fire with our soup boiling above it. This, our first test of the commissarial resources of the boats, proved satisfactory. The rest of the day we paddled through magnificent rocky wooded passes, with here and there an opening showing us some house or a farm couching upon its pasture, and on one island a fine old ruin.

Turned In.

As evening lowered we looked out for some house at which we might put up for the night, but nothing earthly could we see within half a mile of us, large beds of reeds always dividing us from solidity. So we pushed on; and, by every mile of paddling, our chance of finding a house seemed lessened.

At 11 P.M. we determined to go no further, not having tasted food since one o'clock, and the night turning very cold; we had now passed beyond all rushes, and at the same time beyond all hope of houses, the steep rocks bristling to the water's edge. We stumbled on shore in the strange semi-darkness caused by the faded western glow which gives a false appearance to surrounding objects, so that one cannot distinguish where the water ends and the land begins. After many a flounder and bump on the rocks, we succeeded in placing the two canoes side by side, on a flat portion a short distance from the water.

We soon had fire and lamps alight, and soup and coffee under weigh. After supper, we prepared for the night by fixing our mackintosh coats over the hatchways of the canoes, laid a rug on each bottom, and then began the artful dodge of stowing five-feet-eight of man—head and shoulders under the after-deck, legs and feet under the fore-deck, body in the well. This little manœuvre has to be achieved by shoving two-thirds of your body, counting from the foot end, under the forward-deck, and then carefully putting your head under the after-deck, and hauling yourself aft by your hands. Cover the hatch with the mackintosh, leaving a small aperture for air, shove the life-belt under your head, and blow it out into a convenient pillow. This mode of sleeping is very well as long as you are dry; but that night, as on many others, our rugs, coats, trousers, &c., being completely wet, the cold compelled us to rise at three o'clock. Broad daylight, but the mist so dense that we could not see many yards. We climbed the rocks, and found that the fog lay low and heavy along the whole valley of the river. As we had no meat or bread in the storeroom for breakfast, we paddled on, at first cold and shivering, through the soft white veil; but by 9 A.M., when we caught sight of a farmhouse half-a-mile inland, the sun was already burning-hot, the delicate wreaths of vapour had vanished. We walked off to the house, purchased eggs, black bread, and butter, returned to the river, and made our breakfast, then spread sails, clothes, and kits to dry, and we ourselves rolled into the grass for a good sleep.

By midday, thoroughly refreshed, with a rattling breeze and fine weather, we scudded on our course up the river, until we reached the first rapid. On landing we found the river had made a heavy bend, the rapid being off the point. We therefore lifted the boats out, and carrying each in succession, launched them above the rapid. After paddling through long picturesque reaches, and deep quiet pools, which reflected the sun gleaming from between the clouds, we arrived at Lilla Edit, a small village at the last waterfall on the Gotha River, surrounded by saw-mills worked by the cascade. Running parallel to the river is a short canal, with a set of locks at each end, through which vessels are enabled to get above the falls. We found there was a small inn, so had our boats carried into the sitting-room, and indulged in the luxury of sleeping in a house and in a bed. Next day we went to the salmon-fishery, which has fallen off much of late years. We tried for hours with flies and spinning, but fruitlessly. The natives catch them with nets. The current here was too strong to paddle against, to make any reasonable progress. Therefore we determined to await the arrival of the steamboat for Wenersborg, and then to avail ourselves of it thus far. At midnight, the steamer entered the locks. H. and I started from the inn; seizing the *Isis*, we carried her down to the steamer, and were returning for the *Nautilus*, when we met the landlady and her daughter running down the hill at a good trot, with the *Nautilus* under their left arms and bearing the two paddles in their right hands.

CHAPTER III.

FALLS OF TROLLHATTEN—LAKE WENERN—CARLSTAD—A WET RUN.

BY 1 A.M., with daylight approaching, Captain Ericson, who spoke English well, said it was no use to turn in, as we should soon come to the waterfalls of Trollhatten. We therefore made ourselves comfortable on the bridge, enjoying the grand, wild scenery in the dusky morning. The roar of a waterfall became distinct, louder, and heavier, as we neared it, when, on rounding a point, suddenly the glorious sight of the locks of Trollhatten broke upon us: a mountain face, as it were, with locks rising one above another—a stupendous marvel! Vessels stepping up before one's eyes, from lock to lock, to a height of 120 feet from the lower part of the river into the Trollhatten canal above, which deposits them back again in the river, but above the waterfalls. There is a grand old canal, which was blasted and cut through half a mile of solid mountain, forming a huge narrow dyke, with a series of locks along its bottom, but this is now left unused, owing to the still greater work since achieved. When the steamer entered the first lock, we went into the captain's cabin and he regaled us on Swedish punch; we then started ashore to see the falls. All the paths and roads were covered with sawdust, and a mill appeared at every single spot where water could be caught to turn the wheel. In some of these mills they mash great logs of wood into pulp, pack it in casks, and send it away long distances to be finally converted into paper.

The falls consist of a long wild cataract, the water bounding down over stones and rocks, with here and there a large troubled pool whence the same body of water again launches forth, hissing and crashing round and over islands and rocks, forming many channels, again uniting, some having passed through quiet shady pools, whilst others have had it rough all the way, making a last grand leap into the river below, and gliding quietly away to be mixed with the waters of the vast North Sea. We mounted the heights, and rejoined our steamer in the Trollhatten canal, and, after a few miles of the Gotha river, entered another canal, the "Karlsgraf," which takes a short cut across country into Lake Wassbotten, thus escaping another series of falls.

It was not until after entering this Karlsgraf canal that the passengers—some ten or fifteen—began to come on deck. They had slept through all the grand scenery, and were just in time for a fine view of the flat marshes around Lake Wassbotten, a kind of bay of Lake Wenern. Captain Ericson now told us that, after touching at Wenersborg, he was going to Carlstad, and thence on a cruise on the N.W. side of Lake Wenern, and proposed that we should accompany him, promising to bring us back again to Wenersborg, from which town we wished to start in our canoes. To this plan we agreed; and after landing the passengers we enjoyed this fine inland sea, along which we steamed all day. Lake Wenern is the largest lake in Europe excepting Ladoga, being about 100 miles long by 50 broad (in places).

Towards evening we reached Carlstad, built on an island formed by the two mouths of the river Klar, and connected with the mainland by a magnificent bridge. Here we found passengers ready for the cruise awaiting the steamer, and by 10 P.M. we were off again. Next morning we were still steaming on, bound for Upperud, a small village, whence a new series of cuttings are now in course of formation, to connect one lake with another, to gain a direct communication with Christiania; thus it becomes an enterprise of great commercial interest. Through a net-work of lakes, rocky crags, and wooded hills, we at last reached Upperud, where we all disembarked from the large steamer into a small one of about thirty tons, better suited for canal work. In this we proceeded through more lakes until our course was arrested by a waterfall. Here the steamer turned into a set of locks on the right-hand side, which raise boats up into a large iron aqueduct, which crosses the river at the top of the falls, and through which we steamed into the lake above. Here we got ashore, as the water looked good for salmon, whilst the other passengers went on, enjoying a noisy brass band and many tedious locks up to the end of the new canal, where they were to turn round and come back to Upperud. After fishing in the best-looking places for two hours, without one rise, we had the pleasure to learn that there was not a single salmon or trout in the water. So we walked off across the hills, finding our way back to Upperud. There we launched our canoes from the big steamer, and took a cruise amongst the lakes, where we had good perch and pike fishing until evening, when we rejoined the steamer, started for Carlstad, and arrived there early next morning.

Having landed the passengers, we now turned towards the N.E. corner, for a small village, Skattkarr, where we took in a cargo of steel and iron, and returned to Carlstad and Wenersborg. Here the weather continued so dirty that we waited a couple of days hoping it might clear, but this it declined to do, so we could delay no longer, and on the 29th our canoeing life commenced in earnest.

The morning was anything but propitious, a fresh south-westerly wind blowing, the barometer at 29.9, a heavy sea, and every prospect of rain. Our first course lay from the lighthouse at Wenersborg to Cape Udd, about 10 miles, over which we ran before a heavy sea, which increased as we distanced the land, and made sailing impracticable. At Cape Udd we landed on one of the numerous rocky islands—about two acres of thickly wooded mossy rocks, which would have formed a delightful dining-room but for the pouring rain. We soon had a good fire and our dinner cooking on it. All stores and baggage were wet, for what little water there was in the bottom of the boats was well washed about by the heavy seas. The seas were so short we had been unable to use our sails, for, even when paddling easy, we had some difficulty in keeping the boat's nose from running under the sea in front of her, when she would be lifted astern by the next sea, and either be capsized or ship a lot of water, neither of which would be pleasant whilst four or five miles from the nearest land.

During our halt on the island the wind shifted from S.W. to N.E., in a heavy rain-squall, so, for the rest of the evening, we had to paddle against a head-wind amongst numerous islands, on one or other of which we landed several times to take bearings of the headlands in sight, in order to find the position of the canoes on the chart. Waste of work enough we had, for want of a deeper water, or rather for want of a truer and minuter chart to guide us; the result of error involves one in the "square root of a negative quantity." Divers were our errors, and divers were the miniature voyages of discovery we made up small bays which invariably ended in a swamp, yet at last we happened upon one sufficiently flooded to float the canoes across to a bay belonging to the other side of Cape Udd.

CHAPTER IV.

COW "MAKING TRACKS"—NIGHT IN A HUT—"TOUCH AND GO"—IN THE SURF.

No house, no sign of human life, darkness increasing, rain coming on again, we cast about for a moderately dry spot for the night. Presently from out of the forest of fir emerged a woman and a cow. Happy thought! the woman must have some place to sleep in, and, as it is so late, her home may probably be near. I blew my whistle to attract her attention, instead of which it scared her, and off she ran, as fast as she could go into the wood.

We landed as near as possible, hid our canoes in the bush, and made for the forest, but our Atalanta had sped so swiftly as to leave no impress of her foot behind her. Happily her cow was heavier; we discovered its track, followed it, and after a long wander through pine-woods, found a cottage. There we saw a man smoking his pipe, so we approached and asked him, in Swedish, for milk, eggs, and a bed. The whole family turned out, were very polite, and said "ja" to everything we wanted. So we led our host back to show him our boats, and, whilst we paddled round, he, on land, guided us to the next bay, at the head of which was his cottage, to which we had before gained access only by the roundabout track through the forest.

THE "ISIS" RUNNING.

30*th July.*—We started with a heavy sea and fresh breeze from S.W., with double-reefed sails and jibs; and having to cross a good stretch of rough water from one headland to another, we kept our life-belts handy. The seas ran very high; at times I almost lost sight of H. and his canoe, only the top of the mast being visible whilst in the trough of the sea. After about a ten-miles' run we landed on a small island, made up a hut, with sails and branches of bushes, fried the pike we had caught, and made ourselves snug for the afternoon; the gale increasing all the time. Towards evening, the weather not improving, we again got under weigh, but the impetuous blasts urged us to seek some resting-place for the night.

We had not paddled far round the island when we came upon an actual hut, close to the water's edge, evidently built by some fisherman or sportsman. We hauled the boats ashore, opened the door, and found it uninhabited. There, in the corner, was a nice little fireplace, of which we soon made use to prepare supper, and then availed ourselves of this unexpected shelter for the night.

31*st*.—The S.W. gale having increased rather than diminished, we walked across the rocks to the summit of the island, to have a good look at our intended course. We had now to steer to the Hinna-bak, a long reef stretching some five miles at right angles to the mainland. Through this reef, according to my chart, there was a passage, but as Hinna-bak was hardly visible on the horizon, we could not determine much from our present standpoint. We had been repeatedly warned that on Lake Wenern a very heavy sea would get up with a south-west wind. The case had not been overstated, and it was difficult to believe that the waves around us were those of a fresh-water lake, not those of the British Channel, in a gale.

With an area of 2,000 square miles Wenern offers space enough for the continued friction of the wind on the water to raise fine waves, but it looked as though there must have been, furthermore, systems of waves moving with different velocities, whose crests would thus become superimposed upon each other, to produce such a sea as this.

Having stowed the mainsails under the deck, and set our jibs, we ran before the mass of water, but on arriving wet through, at the Hinna-bak reef, we found a dead lee shore, a heavy sea breaking in on to the rocks and no passage. The jibs were in in a moment, as it was evident nothing could be done but paddle round the point, a distance only of about half a mile, which, nevertheless, took us two hours to accomplish. At last, after a narrow escape in running through the tail end of the surf, we got into calm water to leeward of the bak, and hauled the boats up just under the landmark.

We soon made a fire of drift-wood and dried our

clothes. The landmark was a huge three-sided wooden obelisk. At one side some of the boarding did not quite reach the ground, so by clearing away rubbish and stones we contrived to creep in underneath, where we found a spacious baronial hall, but as it was midday, and not midnight, we could not avail ourselves of its hospitable shelter for more than an hour. We now sailed across to the Island of Sparo in Uller Sund; caught some pike and perch and hauled up at a small barn. The people to whom it belonged brought us milk and rye porridge, and seemed delighted at the sight of the boats.

CHAPTER V.

PIKE AND MOSQUITOES—MARIESTAD PRISON— WEST GOTHA CANAL.

AT five next morning, in fine calm sunshine, we continued our journey through the Uller Sund. But gloom succeeded brightness, clouds banked up on every side, a steady downpour commenced and lasted on with zeal deserving of a better cause. From the Sund we emerged on to a broad bay, which we crossed to the little village Hellckis at the foot of the Kennekulle mountain. Here we hauled up in a quiet little cove, cooked our pike, and in vain endeavoured to dry the clothes in the soaking rain. The mosquitoes were very troublesome, biting right through our flannel shirts and trousers whilst we dined under shelter of the fir-trees. The insects and the rain together proved so inhospitable that we gladly pushed on that night to Onas, a village with a glass factory. We were inquiring of the workmen whether there was any place where we could sleep, when three or four gentlemen made their

MARIESTAD.

appearance, and begged us, in German, to come and pay them a visit; so the boats were soon on their lawn and we in their house.

Next day they kindly lent us their open carriage, one of them accompanying us to see the mountain and two gentlemen's houses, with fine grounds and well-laid-out gardens. We also visited the extensive basalt quarries, but as the rain was incessant we did not get a good view from the mountain.

After another comfortable night with our kind hosts at Onas, we started for Mariestad. The sea was running very heavy, barometer low, wind S.W., and blowing in nasty gusts. So, under close-reefed sails, and with nothing worse than a wetting, we ran into the harbour of the little town of Mariestad. A grand procession soon formed up to the hotel, continually augmenting as we were sighted by the small boys and idlers of the place. The hotel was a large new one, and the staircase big enough to allow the canoes to be carried up to a bedroom, where they were safely locked in, and the key given to me.

Next day, on coming out of my door, I was surprised to see a small mob of people issuing from the canoe room. On sight of me, the landlady precipitately locked the door, and vanished into an adjoining chamber, whilst the small mob, after a terrified glance at me, bolted down the stairs. We, however, relieved the landlady by saying that her little exhibition might continue, so long as nobody touched the things.

Whilst walking in the town, a young man came politely up to me, made a series of bows, and asked me in German if I would go and see his sister, who could speak English. I fear it was not polite, but, knowing nothing of him, I replied that the better plan would be for him to bring his sister to the hotel. They came, and she proved to be a very agreeable lady, who kindly showed us all over the town and prison. The prison was on the solitary-confinement system, well built and ventilated. The majority of prisoners were there for forging little bank-notes, worth about 1s. 2d. each. Two or three were in for murder, and will remain there with their heads on until they confess. If once they confess, they are executed. Did time allow, it would be deeply interesting to study the effect of the system pursued here, alike on petty and on aggravated cases.

August 6th.—This morning, our friends in Mariestad informed us that everybody had told everybody else that we were about to leave, and that, therefore, people had been pouring in early to-day from the country to see us start. On quitting our bedroom, we found the hotel full of people, then the market-square full, then the small streets leading to the water so crammed that we could hardly get the boats along. After pushing and shoving through the crowd, we managed to embark, and, on clearing from the shore, found the harbour full of sailing and rowing-boats—all crowded with spectators. We set sail, and left the whole behind, making a quick run for Sjotorp, with a nice steady breeze on the beam. We ran right past the place, so inconspicuous was it; the three lighthouses being partially concealed by trees, we did not observe them, and saw no town. On landing on a rock beyond, however, the bearings of the headland at once proved our error, and a steamer coming out from the canal behind us showed that our compass was right, and that we had overshot our destination.

From this place we entered the West Gotha Canal, which is the only water communication across to Lake Wiken, and so on to Stockholm. This West Gotha Canal was begun in 1793 by private merchants, and was carried on with such zeal that it was actually completed in seven years. The railway from Gothenburg crosses the canal at a small village called Torrboda, where there is an hotel, which we determined to reach that night; and we did so at 11 o'clock, after having had to carry the canoes over many a troublesome lock.

Next morning brought us to Lake Wiken, after a couple of hours paddling and hauling over locks on the dull canal. Three hundred feet above the sea, Lake Wiken, with its fine oaks, offers as beautiful lake scenery as one can wish to behold. There was a dead calm when we entered the lake, and it lasted all day. The scenery was, indeed, picturesque—less wild than that on Lake Wenern, more houses and cultivated country to be seen. Ducks, snipe, divers, and pike were just as plentiful. Towards the east end of the lake, navigation became very intricate, the maps being so inferior, and, owing to the refraction towards sunset, we could not judge of distances. Thus, many a turning that we attempted turned out no go. At last we hit upon the right track, and attained a lock which separates Lake Wiken from Lake Wettern, the latter being a few feet lower.

It was now pitch dark, getting very cold, and as there must still be an hour's hard paddling to reach Carlsborg, we were having a smoke and a glass of grog, to prepare us for our night's work, when we heard a steamer whistling for the lock to be opened. Presently she appeared, and entered the lock. Often as we had to paddle by night in unknown waters, yet there is no need to teach dangers to come on, by over-early buckling towards them, so, as the opportunity for a lift thus offered, we inquired of the captain whether he was going to Carlsborg, and, being answered in the affirmative, shunted the canoes aboard.

CHAPTER VI.

YACHT-CLUB—MOTALA—TOWING CANOES—
LAKE ROXEN.

AFTER we started, however, the captain revealed to us that he did not run to Carlsborg itself, though he could land us off its port, unless we would, as he should prefer, cross over with him to Wadstena, at which place we should arrive in the course of the night.

We took his advice, slept on board, and found ourselves next morning in the little harbour of Wadstena; the steamer was lashed alongside the walls of a huge castle of the sixteenth century, surrounded by a wide moat, branching out of the harbour, acting as docks for the harbour of Wadstena. On leaving him, Captain Owen would not allow us to pay anything for our passage, and kindly gave us a letter of introduction to a friend of his, in charge of the East Gotha Canal.

We remained at Wadstena only till about eleven, then started in our canoes; and, on clearing the crowded shipping, we found awaiting us the Wadstena Yacht Club, consisting of some five or six open boats of three or four tons each, with peculiarly ugly spreet-sails, and a great variety of large flags. These yachts evidently intended to accompany us to Motala. The breakwater was thronged with people right away to the lighthouse at its extremity, and the harbour was covered with well-filled rowing-boats. As soon as we were clear of the breakwater, the largest yacht began to fire salutes from small brass guns. A fine fresh westerly breeze blowing, we soon found that our little canoes could sail round the other boats. The distance to Motala being only about 12 miles, and intending to remain there two or three days, we made no hurry, but had plenty of time to enjoy the beauties of Lake Wettern. This lake is the next largest to Wenern, containing 900 square miles' surface of water. It is nearly 300 feet above the sea, and in some parts 70 fathoms deep, 90 miles from north to south, averaging 15 miles breadth. Only one river runs into it, and only one—the Motala—runs out of it. The scenery is exquisite, and the oak-trees such as one longs to sketch.

The yachts dropped off one by one, until we were accompanied only by the largest, evidently the admiral's ship. We ran in to Motala, and our canoes were soon reposing in the coachhouse of a nice little inn.

The ironfoundries here are the greatest in Sweden,

making engines and other large machinery. We strolled about to see the town, and in the course of the afternoon met about a dozen fellows, the passengers of the yacht. They came up in an open, friendly way, shook hands, made us most polite bows, signifying that they were returning to Wadstena, not a word, however, being spoken on either side, for, alas! all Teutons though we were, *we* proved to be almost as ignorant of their Scandinavian branch as *they* of our Low German branch of the language. It is the glory of the inflectional languages to have reduced all the essential elements to conventional symbols; thus did we, in turn, substitute for language conventional symbols, by means of which we lovingly bade each other adieu.

Next day we called on Captain Owen's friend, who gave us a big official paper—orders to the lock-keepers to pass the canoes, in consequence of which, for the future, we paid nothing at any lock. The Motala river runs into Lake Boren, which is fifty feet below Wettern, though only three miles off. Thus the river is a rapid the whole way, and the banks on both sides are crowded with sawmills, whose water-wheels and barriers form a network over the whole river. Navigation is carried on by a canal at the side, with seven locks to lower vessels into Lake Boren (243 feet above the sea).

August 10*th*.—We left Motala, and after half-an-hour's paddle on the canal, reached the locks. Here we hauled the canoes ashore, dragged them by the head-rope down the grass slopes at a merry trot, and launched them on Lake Boren. We were soon ploughing the water up before a fine south-westerly breeze, and at the end of the lake we entered the East Gotha Canal. Here we paddled for a mile or so to get clear of houses and mills, then hauled the boats into the forest, chose the best shelter under the fir-trees, and had our dinner whilst the rain poured. As there seemed no chance of the rain stopping, we again started, now making use of the tow-path to walk and tow the canoes. This we found a very pleasant variation of the day's work, and as evening approached we came in sight of the church tower of Berg, the top of it flush with the water, owing to the abrupt ending of the canal in a set of thirteen locks, which lower vessels by 130 feet down a steep rocky face into Lake Roxen, 109 feet above the sea. After hauling the boats round three of these locks, we came to the little hotel at Berg, at the top of the steep slope, down which the locks look like a set of steps.

Next morning, when ready to start, we found that the two boys, who had helped to carry the canoes to the hotel the night before, were waiting outside with two wheelbarrows, on which we placed the boats, and all trudged down the path beside the locks. Once launched, a strong breeze soon carried us across the greater part of Lake

Roxen, so we landed on an island, gave the boats a thorough scrub out, washed the sails, dined, and went to sleep. After some three hours we got under weigh, and, tearing along before a freshened breeze, soon reached Norsholm, our halting-place for the night. The lock-keeper here put our boats into the store-magazine, and then accompanied us to the hotel, the most ludicrously small place ever honoured with the name, looking like a miniature Swiss cottage, about 20 feet long by 10 feet high. It consisted of a kitchen and one other room, containing a table and two chairs. We did not, however, remain there, as the lock-keeper kindly offered us two rooms in his house.

CHAPTER VII.

INVISIBLE RIVER—NORRKÖPING—DEER-STALKING AT QVARSEBO.

FROM Norsholm the East Gotha Canal pushes straight on to the Baltic, but we diverged northwards by the Motala river into Lake Glan. This part of the Motala is a varied series of rapids, cataracts, and quiet pools, affording the most beautiful scenery of that portion of Sweden. Here, lofty rocks tower up on either side, stormbrands of ages on their rugged sides; masses of sombre-leaved firs tufting the crags which overhang the river, whilst in other parts the scene changes, and one glides through homely, cultivated lands, bright, grassy meadows, and English river scenery.

The fishing here, as might be expected from the nature of the river, is first-rate. We caught two good-sized salmon trout, several small grayling and perch, but unluckily the best places for fishing were just those where the boats required most management. Three times we had to haul them round cataracts, up and down rocks most peculiarly shaped, for carrying boats over. After the last cataract the river widened, lost its current, and having broken our way through a great bed of tall reeds, Lake Glan, in flood of waters, lay before us.

On pulling into shore we were surprised to find a park-like place full of old oaks. The rain which had been hanging about all morning now came down in good earnest, so we had to paddle under it towards the town of Norköping, which we hoped to reach that night. On arriving at the end of the lake, where the Motala river again runs out, we had much difficulty to find it.

Our map showed it clearly enough, the chart depicting a plain shore with a good broad black river going straight away from it, direct to Norköping; but no such river could we discover, though we found dozens of islands and large beds of reeds, stretching as far as the eye could reach. Our only resource was to mount these islands, look out for the most likely course, paddle through the reeds, climb another rock, and so on. The water varies from 4 feet to 4 inches depth in some places, and the reeds, which grow from the bottom, form an almost uniform height of 7 feet above the water. They grow so close that at times it was difficult to shove the canoes through, and when at last we got past the islands, nothing but beds of reeds could we see,—before, around, and behind us. From the top, however, of one ascent we descried a small piece of clear water, for which we accordingly steered. H. and I soon lost sight of each other in the reeds, and had to ensure some proximity by whistling and shouting, but finally we both shoved through to the clear water, the current of which unmistakably proved it to be the river we were seeking.

WHICH WAY?

Our paddles and the current, together, brought us once more between solid banks, then the music of rapids became distinct, and merrily we rushed down them. After three or four swift descents we came to a number of mills and a small waterfall. Here every man in the place turned out to see us, and our boats were politely carried for us and launched again below the cascade. We were now very close to Norköping, and could hear the waterfall distinctly; darkness was impending, so we hurried at a good pace down the rapids; night advanced, and when it became pitch dark we slackened our pace, floated down with the fast current until, on rounding a point, the lights of mills and of the town of Norköping gleamed before us, and the roar of the water sounding closer than ever, we pulled ashore.

The bank was of great height, covered with large trees; small garden footpaths wound about it in every direction. After wandering along these, up and down the labyrinth in the darkness, to a considerable height, I came out into a gentleman's grounds, and at last to palings and to a safely padlocked gate. As there was no chance for boats to get through that way, I groped my way down again. We then put on our boots and coats, and leaving the canoes, started along the waterside, keeping to one of these small paths, and at last found a gate which was not locked, through which we made our way towards the lights. We addressed the first man we met, and sent him off for three more, who soon carried our boats through the town to the fine hotel at the other end.

At Norköping we remained three days, having at last

reached the shores of the Baltic Sea, some ninety miles only from Stockholm. We were anxious to obtain good charts of the coast: so tried on board all the steamers: they had none to spare; but at last the mate of one introduced me to an office where I was speedily served with two admirable charts of the Baltic Sea and Mälar Lake, at the small sum of two rix dollars = 2s. 4d. We laid in stores of biscuits, tea, and brandy, for our sea-voyage, and started early on a calm rainy morning, with a low barometer. After three miles' final windings of the Motala River, we entered the Brà Viken, a long gulf, the water quite salt, and seaweed surrounding us in place of the water-lilies. The wind rose, and the waves with it: so we had to paddle against a strong head-wind and chopping sea, but by sunset reached Qvarsebo.

We landed, hauled the canoes up, and were preparing for a walk inland, when a small boy made his appearance, and after a good stare, ran away. Shortly he reappeared with his sister, a gazelle-like young lady of eighteen. She immediately asked us in German where we had come from, where we were going, what we called the boats, to what country we belonged, whether such boats were safe, whether we had been far, whether the wind was not too strong for us; in short, she asked fifty questions without waiting for one answer. When she had composed herself by a thorough investigation of the kayaks, we inquired of her whether we might deposit them in the barn for the night. She soon brought out a cottager, and the boats were at once safely housed.

By this time it was dark, and we all walked together up the road, winding in and out of the rocky crags, until we reached a nice little country house; the young lady then gave us full directions for finding the inn, and having earnestly inquired as to the exact time we should start in the morning, she and her brother entered their house.

CHAPTER VIII.

FIRST DAY ON THE BALTIC—A SHOUT IN THE DARK—
OXLÖ SUND.

15*th August.*—Daylight told us more than we had perceived the previous night, and revealed to us two good houses, one inn, four cottages, and several barns alongside the road that we had ascended last evening, down which we now came towards the water, and espied the charming young German lady and her brother. She told us that the inhabitants of the village had been waiting ever since six o'clock to see us start. She, and her brother and sister, were on a visit from Germany to their Swedish aunt and cousins; and on proceeding farther, opposite to their house, we met them all. Remote as was this village, their chignons, and high heels, and paniers, were worthy of Paris. The fair cousin of our German friend, like every Swedish lady we had yet met who could speak English, wore spectacles, and was decidedly out of her teens; with frank and with "uncurbed plainness" she proceeded to interrogate us in English. We endeavoured to satisfy these ladies by giving them a general outline of our cruise, and then wended our way down to the barn. Here were some fifty or sixty peasants awaiting us: so after getting out our boats, still one more lecture was expected.

We now coasted on from headland to headland, and from island to island, until the shores widened, and the clear horizon bounded the circling sea. Towards mid-day the sun's rays becoming powerful, we hauled up under some shady trees, in a pretty little bay. Later on, we again paddled forth; the shores assumed a new appearance—high rugged cliffs and perilous steeps precipitous to the water's edge—whilst in the distance small rocky islands spangled the heaving ocean.

The wind had quieted down—a dead glassy calm lay round us—the only movement or sound to be heard was that of the long ground-swell, rolling in from the southeast, and crashing on the rocks with a low thud like very distant thunder. To land every now and then on those islands was necessary in order to take the bearings and lay off the next course, but easier said than done; for on coming alongside the rocks, we floated at one moment close to a pleasant landing-step, and the next moment we were eight or ten feet below it, and all rock in the wake of the swell was covered with brown slime. The only way then was to watch for the boat rising, and before coming to the summit of its rise, to spring out, hauling the boat instantaneously after one on to the rock above reach of the water. Most of these islands are masses of rock, rising perpendicularly out of deep water, so that if one misses footing and slips, the only resource is to get on board the canoe again, as no one could land from the swimming posture, owing to the slimy and precipitous nature of the rock. This, however, only applies to those islands at a good distance from the shore. Those which form the close network along the Baltic coast are well wooded, with shoal water around, the swell completely broken, and a deep channel winding in amongst them.

The weather now turned thick—so we steered a straight course for the Femörehufvud lighthouse; but the sun had already gone down some time before we sighted it. The lighthouse is a most peculiar building, standing at the extremity of a rocky cape; it consists of a red-stained wooden cottage, with one square white patch on the wall facing the sea; in the centre of the patch is fastened a large camphine lamp, with an extraordinary little chimney starting up the wall, then branching out, to clear the wide overspreading Swiss-like roof. This is the pilot station; but as we paddled, on seeing no one about, we gave a loud Australian "cooee." Immediately two or three men and a woman ran out of the house: then one rushed back, and re-appeared with a telescope, through which they all had a good one-eyed stare at us as we passed round the cape and entered Oxlö Sund. Soon a faint outline of the little village became visible at the end of the Sund. The burden of mist was still upon us, but the dangers of fog were lessened as the moon rose, and we paddled into the bay in the centre of the village.

LIGHTHOUSE ON THE BALTIC.

Not a man to be seen. We landed alongside the little pier, at which steamers call on their way to and from

Stockholm, and hauled the boats up on to it. We then started off to find the inn, and having walked through the village, seeing nothing that looked at all likely to be one, we went up to the door of a cottage on the hill above the landing-place. Our knocks were at last answered by a woman, and to our inquiries for the inn, she exclaimed, "Hyar! hyar!" evidently signifying that she knew English, and meant to say, "Here, here." We returned to the landing-place for our canoes, placed them in the entrance-hall, which they completely filled, and we ourselves entered a large upper chamber with slanting ceiling. On one side of the room was a pile of beds, prepared to make up for any number. Though this proved to be the Grand Hotel of the watering-place of Oxlö, we could get nothing beyond black bread and butter, eggs, milk, and hot water for dinner.

CHAPTER IX.

ORSBAKEN—THUNDERSTORM—NOCTURNAL VISITORS—
CROSS SEAS.

16*th August.*—On waking and looking out of the window, the prospects of the coming day's voyage were not of the liveliest. A strong E.N.E. wind was blowing, and our courses during the day would be mostly in that direction. Paddling against a head-wind is very well now and then; one's arms and body assume a machine-like mode of working, a kind of swing-stroke, which one continues without much thought for almost any length of time; but after luncheon and towards evening one gets impatient at making so little progress, and it becomes anything but pleasant. One feels inclined to go ever so far out of the course to get under the lee of even the smallest rock, just for the change of a moment's smooth water, a lull in the wind, and escape from the blinding spray.

Having crossed the Orsbaken, a broad stretch of water which runs inland some twenty miles to the town of

Nyköping, we passed the Ledskär light, of similar construction with that at Femörehufvud.

From thence, the deep channel which the steamers use, takes a very roundabout course, in towards the mainland: so we made a short cut among the islands to meet the channel again. The whole way we were putting up flights of ducks, geese, and snipe, but were unable to shoot them, simply for want of a gun. The breeze was very fresh, and about midday we hauled up on an island, between which and another, 200 yards off, lay the channel. At its ingress and egress were buoys and landmarks in profusion; and during a couple of hours spent on the island in rest, dinner, and a walk, numerous timber-vessels passed us at a rattling pace with a roaring, scrunching sound, owing to their being clinker-built, and running dead before the stiff breeze, which, in all probability, outside was a hard gale, the wind being sufficient, but the sea here not having room enough to get up.

On leaving this island, we paddled across a long stretch of water: the short seas, being of a thin crested nature, broke over us and gave us a thorough ducking. Then we entered another of the narrow channels, winding in amongst precipitous uninhabited islands, and came out into a large open bay, Tvären, out of the opposite side of which runs Safösund, the pilot-station mentioned to us in the morning. We had just come in sight of this station, about two miles dead to windward, when we observed that the thunderstorm, which had been brewing all the afternoon to leeward, was now working up to windward, and clouds of inky black were stretching round to join the war-clouds gathering on the horizon. As time went on, darker and darker grew the rolling mists, and roofs of a house and barn becoming visible above the rocks of the large island of Ringsö on our right hand, looked tempting enough. Two or three vivid flashes, and then the cross blue lightning seemed to open the breast of heaven. The question was decided. We paddled swiftly into the small bay, ran the boats out on the grass, and had just got our mackintoshes on when the first heavy rain began to fall. There was a peculiarly close feeling, thunderous vapour as a substitute for air, and from the wild look of the sky, and the still wilder appearance of the rocks and trees, as stained with deepest purple, we felt we had done wisely to seek some shelter from the pitiless storm.

We reached the houses; the people stared at us with round wide-opened eyes, reiterating vacantly, "Ja, so—o—o—o—o!" and seemed neither inclined to toil to unravel the mystery of our language nor to open their doors to relieve our wants, the paddles we carried in our hands evidently puzzling and alarming them. At last we invited the men, three in number, to come and look at the boats, after seeing which they readily enough carried them up to the house. We then set to work in a business-like way to lay out our stores on the large table in the general sitting-room, whilst the man and his wife kept back the children and others from entering the room beyond the doorway. Yet all their eyes were upon us, and low whispering followed every one of our actions. We made the woman understand that we wanted eggs, black bread, and hot water; then we walked out in the rain to inspect the barn, as the furniture of the room served to show that the whole family must sleep there.

We found a very nice lower compartment in which to place our boats, and on the first floor a fine hayloft. We stowed the boats away, re-entered the house, and set to work to make tea. Then we gave the men some cigars, and we all proceeded to the next room, in which there was a large fire like that of a forge, sat down and smoked in silence, for they did not understand German, and we did not understand Swedish. On re-entering the large room, we found the beds all rigged up, and the family turned in, having kindly reserved for us one bed, somewhat like an overgrown feeding-trough. But we preferred clean hay and fresh air, and, therefore, lit our lanterns and departed to the barn.

We stumbled up the crazy old ladder, with half its steps gone, and then, to make all secure, hauled it up after us on to the platform. We then opened the kind of wooden window, and tumbled ourselves over a large beam into the hay, taking good care to put out our lanterns. At first, we lay down wet as we were, but finding it uncomfortable, we opened our packs all in the dark, fumbled out a complete change, and somehow got the clothes on with about as much hay inside as out. We fell asleep; but presently H., having shifted his moorings a bit, got under a small hole in the roof, and consequently received the water-spout fed from the thunderstorm still noisily raging. This woke him up, and he, in searching for a better berth, woke me up, and I, trying for change of position, got under another water-spout.

We slept on comfortably enough, however, not caring for the storm, until we were once more aroused by two great wet shepherds tumbling in on to us over the beam. Evidently they had been all night watching their flocks, and expected that we had turned in in the house (probably in their bed). Happily, they soon retraced their steps, shut the door, and we slept on in peace and comfort.

17th.—We had hoped that the thunderstorm of last night must have changed either wind or weather; but no—the north-east wind still blew strongly, and all around looked very gloomy. A drizzling rain set in before we started, and we were delayed by the same kind of chopping seas as those of yesterday, only they became larger now that we were amongst larger bays. Here, too, we met a cross sea, because the wind following the coast line down these bays made their waters run at an angle to the sturdy seas of the channel. Thus by the time we reached Bokö-sund the contentious waves had invaded us to the skin.

Here we got under the lee of the land, the rain and mists cleared off, the sun peeped out and we cast about for a suitable spot for a dining-room. Passing a headland we descried a crevice and ran in through it to a miniature bay; we had already spread our clothes to dry on the rocks, when, on gaining the summit, we discovered a much finer looking spot on a small island beyond; so we re-embarked, paddled off, again spread out our things to dry, and sat down to luncheon. Presently, on wishing to open the bottled beer that we had brought from Oxlö Sund (this part of our trip not affording us any fresh water) the corkscrew proved to be missing: I therefore put my hand behind me to draw, by way of succedaneum, the long knife which I always carry in a sheath in my belt; no handle met my grasp, the very belt itself was gone. Had it been the belt and knife alone, it would not have mattered much, as I had a spare knife in my baggage; but as I also carried on the same belt a leathern pouch containing all my money, I had no alternative but to paddle back to the headland to search for it where first we had commenced the drying operations. There I found it, and we were soon on our way again.

CHAPTER X.

MUNICIPAL DUTIES AT TROSA—HEAD WIND AND SEA—BULLOCK-CART.

FROM Bokösund lighthouse we proposed to make a short cut amongst the islands across to the little town Trosa, on the mainland. This cut off about four miles: the passage in parts broad, but very shallow, was, according to the chart, unnavigable. And for ordinary boats the chart proved to be correct, as we traversed a long fiord with a bright sandy bottom, in some places but a few inches under water, only just enough to float our canoes.

Now and then we had to break through large beds of rushes, exactly similar to those we had met with on fresh-water lakes, and on tasting the water the salt was scarcely appreciable. This was owing to a small river running through Trosa into the Baltic at this point; so we traced the mouth of this little river by following a long straight mud-pier, which, as it nears the town, becomes more stony, until at last it develops into a well-built stone quay. We paddled up the river amongst small cottages, with curious-shaped boats moored to the banks, until the little old wooden bridge, of which we had heard so much, appeared in sight. The Swedes say of a man who has no special occupation that he is " like the Mayor of Trosa, who has nothing to do all day but to fish from the bridge." *Ruhe ist die erste Bürgerpflicht.* The rain was pouring, however, and the mayor was not at his post.

The arrival of two canoes under the bridge of this quiet town caused much excitement in its population: they soon flocked down to what is a mere ditch of some fifteen feet width, though dignified by the name of river. Men were soon summoned to carry the boats up to the little inn, where we found ourselves most comfortable, remaining there for two days.

The greater part of this primitive town lay before the windows of our hotel, consisting of the market-place, divided in two by the aforesaid ditch. Fronting us, at the other end of the square, was the town-hall—a small wooden house, the upper part forming the meeting-chamber, and the lower part being a stable. On the centre of the roof is a peculiar erection—a clock-tower, above which is a steeple surmounted by an overgrown weathercock. The other houses were small stores, like cottages, all built of red-stained wood with red-tiled roofs. Our boats were placed in a kind of shed behind the inn, and locked up. Very soon the people found that the landlady possessed the key, and the usual exhibition commenced.

19th August.—The gale, which had been blowing from the northward and eastward for the last five days, was to-day stronger than ever. As we were under weigh at six, we hoped to be able to reach Södertelge; but on entering the long arm of the Baltic, which stretches inland to Södertelge, we found a short, heavy sea, and met the gale face to face. We first tried along the left shore, hoping to get under the lee of some of the headlands; but as this did not avail, we crossed to the opposite shore, along which were numerous islands. By dodging under the lee of these islands, we advanced pretty fairly, until it became evident that we must cut across again. The water here being shallower, the seas were still shorter than those we first met tossing the white foam from their crests.

After a very wet crossing, we landed on a small island, baled the water out of the canoes, and set ourselves to rights. As we got farther on, the fiord narrowed to the width of the Thames at Richmond. Of course here the seas were quieted down to a mere ripple, though the breeze continued as strong as ever. This state of affairs lasted about four miles, when, on arriving at a pool beyond which the fiord widened again, we landed, and remained a good time under shelter of a couple of rugged pines, through which the wind blew in sudden furious gusts, sinking in the intervening seconds almost to a calm.

We were afterwards lucky in finding a series of small capes in our course: so we were able to paddle to leeward of these: and it was only whilst rounding them that the full brunt of the squalls fell on us: they were often so hard, that, though paddling our strongest, we could make no headway at all; in fact, sometimes were drifted astern. There were still many miles between us and the little village, Ytter Järna, and that was but halfway between our present position and Södertelge; but we knew that there was a small posting-inn at Järna, so we paddled round a headland to where, according to our chart, we ought to find the village of Hölö,—that is to say, a church and two saw-mills; and after a hard tug round the headland we sighted the little pier, hauled up our canoes, and walked inland up to the mills. After strolling about amongst various sheds and workshops, where the men only stared and seemed not to understand our questions, we met with a young fellow, apparently the owner's son, who at once recognized us as the two travelling Englishmen talked of in the papers, and invited us into the house. We told him in German that we wanted a bullock-cart to take the boats a short cut across country to the inn at Ytter Järna. He said he would see to it, and when he reappeared he carried in a tray with Swedish punch and glasses, and invited us to help ourselves. Presently he returned with a large map of Sweden, which he offered us; we looked at it as in duty bound, and told him we had similar ones in the canoes, and then we sat down to await the promised vehicle. After ruminating for a long time, we three, opposite to each other, in somewhat stupid fashion, only uttering a word or two now and then, we ventured to inquire again for the cart; he at once pointed to the map on the table, saying, "Da ist die Karte." Striving to speak with uttermost truth of expression, we particularized bullocks, waggon, &c., which accordingly soon appeared at the door.

The young man and some friends of his walked with us down to the little pier about a mile distant; the canoes were safe as we had left them, though the seas had risen, breaking over the pier, and flinging flakes of foam around. The boats were soon stowed away alongside of one another in a spacious hay-cart, drawn by two bullocks, and away we went along the main road to Ytter Järna.

About halfway there the farmer and his friends passed us in an open carriage and pair, and told us they were going to Södertelge. We soon found that they informed every one on their way that we were coming. We were walking about half a mile ahead of the cart when we saw a large house on a hill, some quarter of a mile from the road. Several people came out of the house: ladies and gentlemen in twos and threes kept pouring out until we wondered how many more could come. When some fourteen or fifteen young people had assembled, then came an old gentleman and his old wife, who closed the procession. At the gate they all stopped, but we walked on till, the creak of our cart-wheels ceasing to sound, we inferred that they had stopped it, and that an exhibition was going on. We walked back and saw that such was the case. Two or three similar scenes occurred before the canoes reached the inn at Ytter Järna.

CHAPTER XI.

IN FOR THE "LADY'S MONTH"—STICKY WATER—LUNCHEON AFLOAT.

ON the way we had passed a curious triangular wooden frame, leaning up against a tree. Our driver told us that it was used in winter-time, being then drawn along by five or six bullocks, to plough the snow off and throw it on each side into a ready prepared ditch, some twelve feet wide and eight or ten feet deep. All along, on either hand, at intervals, are large poles fifteen feet high, with bunches of dead fir tied at the top, useful for indicating the course of the road when the snow is deep and the ditches become bridged over with snow: otherwise any one might drive on to the false bridge and fall right through into the chasm beneath.

20th August.—The barometer was still rising, the breeze reduced to a fresh one. In very heavy rain we walked down to a promontory, whence we had a view of the fiord. There was evidently a good stretch of water under the lee of a large headland; and according to the chart there were three or four similar headlands beyond: therefore the wish to reach the town of Södertelge in good time out-balanced the objectionable downpour. We

Snow Plough.

had our boats carried down and launched on the little stream, which here runs into the fiord, winding through marshy land covered with a few inches of water.

We were soon away on the fiord, with a delightful hissing of heavy rain all round; and having broken our way through a bed of high rushes, we entered the calm water to leeward of the headland. Even here the swell rolled in, and, joined with the heavy rain, gave the water a peculiar appearance in the distance,—showing one distinct long line for each swell. We had a hard buffet to and fro against the conflicting wind and rain until we rounded the next headland. A change, however, was approaching: though still raining hard, the heavy gusts of wind blew only at longer intervals, and wide blue patches of sky became visible. The wind died away altogether, leaving us still the heaving swell and the pouring rain. By degrees even this too cleared off and all was steaming in the sun.

When we were at Wenersborg, the captain of the steamer *Udderholme* had warned us that we had come a month too late as regards weather. We were just in for the "Lady's month," during which the Swedes expect incessant rain. It is thus termed because every day of it bears a lady's name. Though there were fine intervals, we certainly had equal to one month of rainy days in the course of six weeks. As both our watches had refused duty, we had not the remotest idea at what time we had started from Ytter Järna, nor at what time we reached the Södertelge canal, uniting a deep inlet of the Baltic, the

Järna fiord, with an arm of Lake Mälaren. This lake, commonly called Malar, is a few feet above the level of the Baltic: therefore we found two locks; but they being in the middle of the town of Södertelge, we hauled the canoes out, and had them carried up to the hotel.

The Malar lake, 75 miles long, differs much from those we had traversed, the name indeed covers a vast tract of country, but owing to the numerous islands (some 1,400), many of which are large, there is scarcely a spot of two square miles of clear water surface.

21st.—Morning broke with a dull leaden sky, looking as uninviting as it well could do; but there being a dead calm, we thought it a good opportunity to slip on to Stockholm with only a ducking. After paddling some miles, the rain cleared off, the sky brightened, and all became fine.

Yet there was a strangely dull feeling about the canoes; they seemed to hang in the water as if they were full of water. Hard strokes made no great difference, and there was little pleasure felt in paddling. There was no wind, a dense steam all round, everything wet and clammy. I cannot even now satisfy myself as to the cause of that dead feeling in the boats. Was it the result of the heavy atmosphere and vast amount of rain water? or was it the sudden change to fresh water, after the last seven or eight days' paddling on the more buoyant-swelling salt waves of the Baltic?

LUNCHEON AFLOAT.

Still some ten miles short of Stockholm, we now heard the lively rattle of paddle-wheels, and espied one wreath of black smoke and many curls of greyish blue smoke, which clearly showed that we were nearing the regular track of the steamers: the black smoke probably belonging to a Baltic boat, and the blue smoke to the small wood-burning screw-launches, which carry passengers in all directions around Stockholm and the various small towns on the Malar Lake.

A light breeze sprang up right aft: we set sail, and took the opportunity, whilst free from paddling, to eat a meal—stretching ourselves at full length, legs on the foredeck and head supported on the back-board: a bottle of beer between the knees, a thick round of black bread, like oat-cake (doubled over, with meat and butter between, forming a huge sandwich), gracefully reclining on the chest, to be nibbled at, whilst one hand steered and the other hand acted waiter with the beer. This luncheon *sub dio* was highly applauded by the passengers on board the steamers, who handed their opera-glasses from one to another, peering as if they would not lose sight of a crumb.

This part of the lake seemed overstocked with perch, for after luncheon, on shaking the crumbs off the paper which had contained the monster sandwich, a great splashing occurred a little astern of the boat, which caused me to sit up and look round. I saw a small naval engagement going on for the crumbs, so I threw out bits at intervals to a complete shoal of perch, who kept company with the canoes. At each large piece several big fellows would make a simultaneous rush at it, banging their heads together, and fighting viciously for the lump, which was too large for any one to swallow. Having been some days on salt water, our fishing-tackle was stowed away, so we caught none of our followers.

CHAPTER XII.

STOCKHOLM FROM THE MALAR—EXPERIMENTS—
OUR SPECIAL ARTIST.

AFTER winding in and out of large islands, we suddenly came upon the noble sight of Stockholm, some three or four miles distant. Nothing can be more striking than the first appearance of this Venice of the North—a glorious city in the sea, one galaxy of spires, churches, many a pile and stately portico, bridges, vessels, land and water.

The large stone bridge leads from the palace to Gustav Adolf Square, in which is the Rydberg Hotel: so we steered down the rapid current towards it. A gentleman in a boat called out in English that we could not go that way, the current being too strong. Judging, however, from the appearance of the water, and seeing a boat pulling across below the bridge, we resisted his advice, turned our boats round, and so drifted down till opposite the stone steps up the high granite embankment. Here we hauled our boats out, placed them on the shoulders of four porters, who carried them across the square into the hotel. But next day's *Aften Blatt* told a different yarn: "The two Englishmen of whom we have spoken before, as travelling through Sweden with their canoes, have arrived in the capital, and landed on the south side of the Gustav Adolf Square. As soon as the travelling gentlemen had landed, they drew their boats out of the water, and taking them under each arm, they promenaded the city."

One morning, two members of the British Legation called on us at the Rydberg Hotel, and expressed much interest in the canoes: they inquired into the state of our rigging and working more practically than do ordinary visitors, who go away as happy as larks after casting a general glance over the whole, and tapping with their knuckles at the deck to discover whether the boat is hollow. These gentlemen kindly invited us out to their place, to see a canoe which one of them had just got over from Searle's. Accordingly, two days later, we started in our canoes to spend a long day with them.

After sailing down the first fiord, the breeze freshening fast and puffy, about four or five miles from Stockholm we saw a cutter beating up to windward, with her main-tack triced up. She must be English, as all the boats here lace their mainsails to the boom. On sighting us she hoisted the British ensign, and proved to be the cutter-yacht *Brenda*, belonging to Mr. G., who had come out to meet us, leaving his friend Mr. J. cruising in his canoe in the other fiord, in which their houses are situated.

As the yacht would run much faster than the canoes, we got on board and towed them astern; but as the breeze freshened and the seas got up, the canoes began to steer badly, sheering from side to side, and running their noses under water. Two or three times the *Nautilus* ran her nose under the quarter of the dingy, also towing astern; the last time she half capsized, and took in a quantity of water, which, rushing aft as soon as she was clear of the dingy's quarter, swamped all my shore-going clothes. (During our cruise in the wilder portions of the country we had worn nothing but flannel, and sent a portmanteau on to await us at Stockholm.) So the yacht was hove-to whilst we hauled the *Isis* on to her deck, and the *Nautilus* into the dingy, where I soon baled out of her eight or ten felt-hatsful of water. We then bore away, and had a pleasant sail down the fiord until we rounded a cape and sailed, close-hauled, up another fiord, at the head of which were the pretty little Swiss-like houses of our friends.

We now sighted the new canoe; the anchor was dropped, and we all paddled ashore. After being most hospitably entertained, we slept on board the yacht.

Next morning we tried various experiments in Mr. J.'s canoe with my sliding gunter-rig, which answered perfectly in every way. We also practised getting into the canoes after capsizing ourselves in deep water. It is a very simple and useful manœuvre: for if a man was to get capsized at sea, several miles from land, and had not the knack of getting in again, he would soon get cramp by holding on to his boat, and must in the end drop off. The way I practise it is this: capsize myself, not being in too great a hurry to get out, otherwise one gets entangled in the sail, which, with the mast, comes adrift from the boat. In short, slide out, seal-fashion, swim alongside, bale her out with your hat, go to the stern, shove it between your legs; lift yourself along the deck, and vault both legs into the hatchway; finish baling out, re-step the mast, and sail on as right as before. As I have never been capsized, except for practice, I cannot say that this plan may do for all weathers, or for all places; but nevertheless it is well to practise it.

We returned to Stockholm, sailing with a stormy northerly breeze on our beam, with quick heavy squalls, which came down without a warning sign off the rocky land. To sail thus was more tiring than it would have been to paddle; for during a squall, even when sitting right over to windward and leaning the body farther still, with the sheet eased off, there was yet a third of the deck under water, including the lee-side of the apron, at the angle of which a nice little trout-stream was running in, as it seems impossible to close in the corners accurately enough to render them water-tight.

28th August.—I went to the railway-station to measure the baggage-van to ascertain whether the canoes could go thus by rail from Stockholm to Malmö. At first none of the railway-officials could understand a word; but afterwards, on taking out my log-book and making a sketch of a canoe, they all seemed suddenly enlightened; then I drew two men in the act of carrying it, and wrote alongside, "50 lbs. weight." Then I depicted a sail and a paddle, and inquired from the most intelligent-looking man what was the fare first-class to Malmö? He said something, but as I was not quite sure of the sum, I wrote down interrogatively, "50 rix dollars?" at which they all shouted "Ya, ya." Then one of them produced a measuring-tape and began to measure the baggage-waggon; finally, we parted upon a mutual good understanding, my small diagrams having been the artificial yet effectual instruments for the utterance and intercommunication of human thought.

CHAPTER XIII.

CARLSKRONA HARBOUR—ARRIVAL AT MALMÖ—BATHS.

NEVERTHELESS, that evening, in one moment, all our plans were changed. Whilst waiting for a summons to dinner, a friend read out of the newspaper that a steamer was going next morning to Malmö. A steamboat is always preferable, for the canoe's sake, to a railway; so immediately after dinner we drove to the office, took tickets, bought charts of the "Sound" and of the Danish coasts, tumbled all our things into the canoes, and had them carried on board the *Svea*.

29th August.—At 8 A.M. the steamer left Stockholm, with a fresh N.N.W. breeze, and some twenty Swedish passengers, who seemed to enjoy fully the sea-air and well-spread mess-tables.

Every meal on board was like a long substantial dinner, commencing with schnapps, black bread and butter, small rawfish or salmon; then soups, fish, meats, puddings, preserves, beer, and schnapps *ad libitum*.

As evening advanced, the decks gradually became clear of passengers. As most of them were "early birds," they sought the "downy" before 8 P.M., and would open their "weather eyes" and poke out their "lee legs" about 4 A.M.

30*th*.—About mid-day we entered the large deep harbour of Carlskrona, and landed at the little town, built on a remarkable set of islands connected by bridges, and surrounded by dozens of smaller islands and rocks, on most of which is a masked battery.

Charles XI. may claim the distinction of having originated this fortification in 1680, and he removed the national fleet from Stockholm here. All through the last century enormous sums of money were being expended in hollowing docks out of the solid rock, and by degrees it has been thoroughly fortified, and converted into the grand naval harbour and dockyard of Sweden. We took the steward of the steamer to ask leave for us to go over the dockyard. Permission was soon obtained, and a very curious collection we saw of ships, boats, old guns, and portions of worn-out vessels. There were three old 10-gun brigs on which boys are trained, and several gun-boats propelled by thirty or forty oars each, which, in the event of an enemy approaching, would be pulled behind one of the small rocky islands, and over this shield the enemy would be attacked. In another portion of the docks we found two Minotaurs, the most remarkable of which is the *John Ericson*, armed with two heavy guns in one turret. Her very low freeboard makes her a difficult object for the enemy to hit, yet deteriorates her qualities as a sea-going vessel.

About 30 miles farther west, the steamer called in at a small fortified town, Carlshamn, where we stopped for about an hour. Ship-building seems to be the chief business of the place.

31*st.*—We passed the light-ship *Falsterbo* early, and about noon we were off Malmö lighthouse. After rounding the buoys, we steamed slowly up the harbour, and made fast to the quay. Here we took leave of the steamer, and having launched the canoes, we started on a cruise along the moats which surround the town. We paddled round the harbour, which has been formed artificially; then had the canoes carried up through the town to the nice little hotel.

A heavy N.N.W. gale was blowing all day, and consequently the "white horses" were numerous outside the harbour.

September 1*st.*—The wind had somewhat lulled, but the weather was still too threatening to make it wise to cross to Copenhagen in the canoes.

A gentleman to whom we had a letter of introduction kindly gave us two tickets of admission to witness the great swimming *fête*, at which the ceremony of granting "Degrees of Doctor of Swimming" was to take place.

To the east of the harbour, about half a mile along the coast, is a large swimming-bath, built on piles, standing well out into the sea, yet guarded from heavy seas by a breakwater and outlying sands, and reached by a long wooden bridge. This place was now gaily decked with flags of all nations, arms, mottoes, crests brightly painted and encircled by wreaths of evergreens, festoons of leaves in all directions.

On the sea-front of these baths a high platform was erected some 20 feet above the water; this was to serve as a diving-board. There were two huge barges moored to posts at right angles to the two sea-front corners, leaving a square space of sea-room for the bathers.

CHAPTER XIV.

"DOCTOR OF SWIMMING"—DROWNED RATS—
BRASS BAND.

ABOUT 4 P.M. people began to arrive in great numbers, so I sailed the *Nautilus* round out of the harbour, and moored her at a convenient distance from the scene of action, whence the whole proceedings could be better observed than from any portion of the baths.

A brass band took up a commanding position on the top of one of the towers at the corner of the building. Soon the place became crowded, the barges were full, and the band struck up.

A boat now made its appearance on the scene, with an overgrown Swedish ensign flying at her stern, and a long pennant at the bows. In the stern-sheets stood a man in full evening dress, tail-coat and white gloves, one arm completely strung with wreaths.

The swimmers came forward on the platform. They

consisted of about fifteen to twenty men and boys, from the age of thirty down to ten. They were all dressed in white shirts, collars and black neckties, and short bathing-drawers. This costume had a most peculiar appearance whilst they were swimming about, each man's shirt forming a sort of white bladder behind his head, and when they came out of the water there was a drowned-rattish look about them ludicrous to behold.

A good deal of diving and various swimming feats and high somersaults took place; then a man dressed as a woman appeared on the platform, and dived off and swam about with ease, notwithstanding the petticoats. They then all formed in a line, "treading water," whilst the band played a short slow march, and, one at a time, each man swam to the flag-boat and was crowned with a wreath. Then the band recommenced the same march as the next man swam up, and a 3 or 4-pounder gun was fired at the moment of each wreath being placed on the head. So it went on throughout the whole number, until, every swimmer being adorned, the whole mass swam to the steps. Here ended the first portion of the ceremony.

Everybody then cleared out, and the greater number adjourned to the hotel, where a grand banquet in the ball-room was to follow. Man being the sole mammal ungifted with the natural faculty of swimming, doubtless needs crowns, degrees, and banquets to incite him to the difficult art.

In the evening, just as we had finished our *tête-à-tête* dinner in the *salle*, our friend, who was the head swimming Doctor, came in with a wreath on his head, and invited us into the banquet-hall. Here we found a large assemblage, in full evening dress, the swimmers still conspicuous by their green wreaths.

The noisy brass band had taken up its position in a kind of magnified swallow's-nest balcony, whence it blurted out occasionally its most extraordinary strains.

The table was abundantly spread with Swedish punch, and the hundreds of guests, all standing up, with glasses in their hands, gave the Swedish version of "three cheers" as each speech ended.

Then commenced the presentation of certificates, beginning with the highest degree, the certificate enumerating all the feats the recipient could perform, the distance he could swim, and the time he had devoted to learning.

As each man thus received his Doctor's degree, the band in the pigeon-hole gave out three blurts, which were immediately followed by three hurrahs. Four or five grandees added a few congratulatory words to each Doctor, which were also followed by three grunts from the band, and three responsive cheers. When everybody in the room had drunk nearly everybody else's health, and all seemed mutually satisfied with each other, and with the proceedings of the day in general, they began to depart, the room by now being so full of smoke, that one could scarcely see across it, cigars having been handed about *ad libitum.*

CHAPTER XV.

TIN HATCH—BOUND FOR COPENHAGEN—A NORTH-WESTER.

I HAD determined to have a tin hatch made for the *Nautilus*, as I thought it would be stronger than the old mackintosh apron, in the event of a heavy sea breaking on to it whilst crossing the Sound. The difficulty became how to explain to the tin-smith what I wanted; as my ignorance of his new Norse language rendered me unintelligible to him, and the Swedish waiters at the hotel were equally at fault. But a sketch soon had the desired effect. I drew the well of the canoe, then the hatch, then in detail small portions of the hatch which required particular attention, such as the beading on the combing. In order to comprehend a picture at all, one must grasp it as a whole: so I added the representation of a man paddling; my tin-smith grasped the whole idea, and off he went to set about this strange order.

3rd September.—The wind had gone down considerably

during the night, and when I went to bathe in the sea, I found the wind had shifted and was blowing a light breeze from the N.E., though there was still a lumpy sea left by the late N.W. gale. Now seemed the opportunity to slip across the Sound before another gale could brew, as it looked fishy to the northward and westward.

On returning to the hotel I immediately sent a fellow off to hurry the tin-smith up with the hatch, whilst I got everything into thorough working order, oiling the mast, gunter-brass, crutches, &c. Every minute being of value, I too followed round to the tinman's shop, and found that he had finished *my* hatch, but that his men were employed in making another, evidently on speculation; that man will thrive.

By 10 A.M. I had taken my last foot off the last stone of Sweden, and was picking my canoe's way amongst a large fleet of herring-boats, all tacking to and fro in the harbour of Malmö, trying to get out against a light breeze, which to my surprise I found had already shifted back to the N.W. The sea, that emblem of uncertainty, had already altered since the morning dawn, and as my first course, from Malmö lighthouse to the north point of Saltholm, was N.W.$\frac{1}{2}$W., this was an ugly change; for I now had to paddle head to wind and pitch and dive over a lumpy sea, instead of running at the rate of five or six miles an hour before the N.E. breeze of the early morning.

The shoals off Malmö run out a considerable distance, so that it was not till I got on to deep water that the fine massive swells were properly felt.

For some time it was pleasant, pitching and diving over these hillocks of water, but by degrees it became very evident that the inky sky, with its little frayed-out cotton-wool clouds, was creeping up " slow but sure " from the N.W. horizon. Also the wind was freshening by jerks, fits, and starts: every now and then a sharper gust came, and only partially lulled away, so that each augmented the previous gust, until at last a stiff breeze was blowing. The sea, which had hitherto been only humpy, became crested, and took the form of regular instead of confused seas.

At this time two fine steamers passed about two miles to the northward of me: the white spray flying from their bows showed that even they began to feel the seas. They were bound for Copenhagen, and I was pleased to see that they were steering the same course that I was, *i.e.* to the northward point of Saltholm, whereas the tracks on the chart all go round the south end. This island is about two-thirds of the way across the Sound.

By degrees it came on to blow so hard, that whilst one blade of the paddle was in the water, it was difficult to push the other forward in the air against the wind.

The seas now went roaring along in proper style, and

some marvellous acrobatic feats were performed by man and boat. Now and then a desperate stroke ahead or astern just saved us from a capsize; then the boat would lift on the crest of a sea and give a kind of forward bound, buoy herself, then rise and shake it all off again.

These little jokes were all very well, but the fruits were, that a great deal of water found its way inside the boat, and it was soon evident that a periodical baling-out would have to take place. Therefore the course must be shifted, for, whilst hove-to the first time to sponge out, she drifted a considerable distance to the southward. This I rectified by steering a point to windward of the course, heaving-to to bale out whenever the water in the bottom of the canoe was above the floor-boards.

After paddling a long time, I became impatient at not sighting the island, fearing that I had allowed too much northerly course, and so perhaps passed it; however on I went, always hoping to see something of it, and found that though the seas were still sharp, the swell became smaller and the heavy plunges fewer.

Presently sea-weed was floating around, and on catching hold of a piece, I found that it was fast to the ground; this was re-assuring. After a little more paddling, on looking down, the bottom was clearly visible, yet no island in sight and a clear horizon right round, excepting only a distant blue tinge astern of the highland of Sweden.

CHAPTER XVI.

CROSSING THE SOUND—SWAN CHASE—SLEEP ON SALTHOLM.

PRESENTLY, right ahead, about ten yards from the canoe, was a grey buoy rising and falling, floating on the swell; and, as I knew that there ought to be no such thing in my course, I reached out the chart to see where I could possibly have got to.

On looking up again from the chart, I saw that the buoy had turned round, and now showed itself as the face, head, and shoulders of a beautiful seal. I jammed the chart away below, paddled quickly towards him: he waited till I got within a couple of yards, then quietly, smoothly went under, and as I passed over the spot I saw him disappear among the seaweed below.

Almost immediately after this, I observed something brown on the horizon right ahead, and as I was now in comparatively smooth water and making better way, this brown object rapidly rose, and soon proved to be the roof of a barn. I immediately shoved the hatch forward and stood up; there lay the long, low, flat island of Saltholm with this solitary barn upon it. Of course it was only owing to sitting so low on the surface of the water, that I had not sooner sighted it. I fetched the island about a quarter of a mile to the southward of the north point, thus proving the correctness of my allowance in the course for leeway. After paddling on again for some time, and nearing the shore rapidly, I saw a fine large white swan swimming along, and half a mile further a man wading up to his waist in water, carrying a gun, evidently in chase. Not far from the man was a sailing-boat, hove to, because of the shoal water. She had a close-reefed mainsail, and a storm-jib about the size of a pocket-handkerchief.

I paddled straight to the swan, to cut off his escape and head him back towards the man, but on getting near found I could overtake him so easily, that I went at him and tried to strike him with my paddle; he was too sharp, he doubled suddenly, and my boat shot past. I was soon after him again, and this time with more success, for I hit him on the back of the neck. I could not hit very hard with only a light paddle and seated so low, the stroke had not much effect; so he turned round savagely, showing fight: I backed clear of him and was preparing for another attack, but turning the canoe too quickly, lost my paddle overboard and nearly "turned turtle."

By the time I had worked back with the footboard and recovered my paddle, the swan had made good tracks in the direction of the man. When within some twenty yards of him the swan suddenly turned and flapped and swam out to sea, the man fired and the shot cut the water up, two or three yards wide of the mark. The pursuer then regained his sailing-boat, shook out a reef, and gave chase, while I landed.

I soon had all my things spread out to dry in the sun, and seated myself to leeward of a rock with a bottle of beer and a good store of biscuits, enjoying at the same time a splendid view of the exciting swan chase. The men in the boat had now shaken out a second reef, set a larger jib, and were ploughing up the water in chase of the swan. Every now and then they had a shot at him, but invariably missed, showing far too much sail to the gale, the boat diving her head under and plunging about in a most reckless manner. At last, however, they winged the bird, and bearing down upon him, one of the men knocked the brave fellow on the head with a boat-hook, picked him up; they reefed again, and were soon lost to sight round the northern point of the land.

The whole island presented a flat, level, grassy plain, and the highest point, independently of the barn, was a mud wall enclosing a small field, the top of the wall being about ten feet above the level of the sea. There

SLEEP ON SALTHOLM.

were hundreds of cattle grazing in the centre of the island. I could discern a large pond, evidently rain-water, as the cattle stood drinking in it.

Being now at peace, in sole possession of the island (entirely cutting Robinson Crusoe out, as I was only there for a pleasant rest; came there of my own free will, in a staunch little ship, and could leave in the same whenever I liked: also no ignorant "Friday" requiring a mental school-board to "bring him up in the way he should go,") I laid down and pondered, enjoying a well-flavoured "weed." I thought over my recent passage from Malmö, then of nothing in particular, but everything in general, then forgot, and tried lazily to remember what the last thought was; the sun and wind were warm, it was very pleasant, the cigar had been for some time smouldering in the dry grass, thoughts had all mutinied and the body had "piped down:" I rolled over, and whether I snored or not there was nobody to hear.

CHAPTER XVII.

MIRAGE—TICKLISH FOOTING—SEALS—HARBOUR AFTER DARK.

FEELING a cold trickling sensation on my face and round my neck, I awoke; rain was falling from a passing cloud, the wind had gone down considerably, and on looking in the direction of Copenhagen, I was surprised to see the town in full view, and vessels sailing along the channel, whereas hitherto I had only seen a dark line of distant lowland.

Looming in a higher stratum of air than they had any right to, were the upper portions of steeples and buildings, and the ships in the Sound, all elevated by terrestrial refraction high above the horizon. The day was certainly one likely to engender mirage: the temperature had been so irregular throughout the morning that it might well affect the density of the air. It secured me one advantage, enabling me afterwards to steer direct for Copenhagen without any reference to the compass.

TICKLISH FOOTING.

I had no sufficiently accurate test by means of which to ascertain whether the refraction was confined to the same vertical plane: there may have been some lateral deviation.

I stowed everything back into my boat and paddled on to the northern end of Saltholm, the water as I neared this point becoming shallower and shallower, until I was in about six inches of water, whilst at least a quarter of a mile from land. I measured the depths by the monogram on my paddle.

The end of the island forms one long stretch, perhaps a mile, of detached rocky islets not more than a foot or two above water, and the passages between them only two or three inches deep: there was every opportunity excepting one for making a short cut across between these, but that one drawback was serious, the bottom consisting entirely of such angular sharp flints that they would cut one's feet to pieces, in the event of wading barefooted to lighten the canoe's draught of water: I did not wish to use the boots which must be worn on landing, and all my other gear was crossing by steamer. I tried several times so far as to put one foot out, but each time, on touching the bottom, the sensation of standing on the top of a wall well stuck with broken glass, caused me to draw it in again. At last a passage somewhat deeper than the rest was found, so I put on my stockings and waded it, the operation not being at all comfortable. I was just getting into my ship again, when another of the small islets, as I thought it, some distance off, began to separate, and I found it was an immense flight of wild-fowl. Having no pistol with me, that also being with my heavy baggage on board the steamer, it was useless to chase them: so I stepped my mast and set "all plain sail."

After cruising about a mile along the north-west coast, I saw a number of black dots ahead, and on nearing them they proved to be seals asleep on small rocks. Being under sail with a light breeze, the boat made no noise gliding through the water. I passed close to one, which did not wake up until the creak of my little mast-head-block, when I topped the boom up to have a good view of those ahead, suddenly roused him: he plunged into the water: this caused a general commotion among the others, and also a number from below soon showed their smooth heads and large eyes above water. I now bethought me to try the dodge of whistling; when a great number of them had dived and my Phocidæan audience was not sufficiently large, I blew a dog-whistle and rapped with the paddle on the sides of the canoe; three or four heads at once appeared above water, and then some more, eyeing me with the most puzzled attentive look.

I sailed on for Copenhagen, now some four miles distant. After several tacks and passing amongst numerous vessels of all nations, I just fetched under the stern of a large French frigate, lying in the roads, when the wind, which had been gradually sinking, died away altogether; so I unstepped the mast, stowed it below, paddled in the direction of the harbour till I was clear of the shipping, and then, dropping the paddle into the side crutch, I lay back with legs on fore-deck and head on the back board, and enjoyed a quiet pipe in the warm glow of the setting sun, and on the pleasant heave of the long ground swell.

By the time I reached the harbour the sun had gone down, darkness came on, and it was very difficult to find the way. The harbour was crowded with ironclads, old men-of-war, merchant-ships, hulks, steamers, and fishing-boats: cables, warps, and hawsers stretched from vessels to buoys and piers in all directions; confusion and chaos around, one came unawares upon the floating flat buoys hardly an inch above water, at once invisible and unavoidable in the dark.

On arriving at a large landing pier, pretty well crowded with people, several of them inquired the name of the canoe; when I had answered, I heard them repeating one to another, "*Nautilus* and *Isis;*" I, having only mentioned the *Nautilus*, knew at once that they must have seen the *Isis*, probably when she was being carried up that morning through Copenhagen to the hotel. So, unconsciously they informed me that she had arrived; and I, on spec, asked to which hotel had she been carried; several voices exclaimed "Phœnix Hotel!" I engaged the two best looking men to carry her up, and the *Nautilus* was soon alongside the *Isis* in the hall of the "Phœnix Hotel."

CHAPTER XVIII.

COPENHAGEN—THORWALDSEN—KIEL HARBOUR—
PRUSSIAN FLEET—HAMBURG.

5*th September*. — Copenhagen, like nearly all the towns at which we had touched, is built on islands, forming harbours and canals. The mouth of the principal harbour is very narrow, but the interior is able to contain nearly a thousand vessels. The houses are well built, the chief streets wide, several very fine public buildings and churches, and the entire city is enclosed within bastioned walls and deep wide moats.

We went carefully through Thorwaldsen's Museum, a remarkable monument of one man's energy; the grand building filled from end to end with his works; he himself being buried there in the midst of them. Thorwaldsen was the son of a carver, and commenced his career as a sculptor in the noble line of cutting "figure-heads" for the Danish shipping.

How rarely does a country show such tender appreciation of any living son, as did Denmark, when publicly sending out a frigate to bring Thorwaldsen from Italy, in state, to Copenhagen.

We left Copenhagen by the night train, with the *Nautilus* and *Isis* comfortably stowed in the luggage-van, on the top of some sacks of meal. About midnight we arrived at Corsor, whence we embarked on a steamer for Kiel.

It rained hard all night; the canoes got full of water and blacks from the steamer's funnels. Below, things were nearly as bad: as soon as the train had stopped, everybody made a headlong run for the steamer, where the order of the day was, first come first served, so that when we arrived, having been delayed with our canoes, we found supper nearly done, and no nocturnal accommodation; there were but eight or ten "bunks" and two sofas, amongst thirty or forty passengers: so we turned in on the cabin deck with spare sofa-bolsters, hard as a brick, for pillows.

6th.—The "early birds" were up by 4 A.M., talking, spluttering, and splashing, as they washed; then lighting their pipes as they dressed, they were soon on deck; it was getting daylight, and "turn out" being everywhere the fashion on board, we followed it.

About five o'clock we entered the harbour of Kiel; after passing the outer forts we steamed between two lines of the Prussian fleet, which, like many another fleet, showed a goodly amount of washed clothing hanging up to dry; but it also exhibited three fine iron-clads, the *Kronprinz*, *Wilhelm*, and *Friedrich*. The port itself is well kept, and the whole is guarded by fortifications on the heights commanding the entrance, whilst torpedoes are ready prepared to check adventurous enemies, who might wander in on seeing so large a harbour, with a tempting craft or two, all ready to be "cut out." It is about three miles long by one broad, and with a depth of forty feet.

The town itself is small, but well built and walled.

Having now entered a new country we met with a new style of officials, and these insisted on having their own way; nothing would persuade them to allow our canoes to be carried by passenger train, and thus it befel that though we ourselves reached Hamburg that morning about eleven o'clock, the canoes never arrived till the evening of the following day.

Hamburg, with its perpetual intersection of water, canals, as well as the Elbe and its tributary the Alster, is just the place for canoeing; and the "Kronprinz Hotel," at which we stayed, being close to the Alster Lake, only divided from it by a boulevard, suited us fully.

This lake runs for some miles into the country, and on its banks are pretty villas and grounds; the scenery much like that of one or other bank of the Thames above

Teddington. Every here and there were moored cutters, yawls, and centre-board yachts with good-looking hulls, and, in many cases, well kept, but all clumsily rigged and fitted. Here, too, were little high-pressure screw-steamers, like those at Stockholm, excepting that these had deck-houses instead of awnings. All round the town-portion of the lake were boats, barges, and hundreds of boats "for hire," yet out of all these there was not one of neat light build: there were many long club boats which pulled from eight, ten, to twelve oars. Most of the sailing-boats were rigged with settee sails.

CHAPTER XIX.

STREAM WORK—ALSTER LAKE—SUNK! BUT ALL HANDS SAVED.

ONE day I devoted to a most delightful sail up the Alster river; it was blowing a N.W. gale at sea, so that I had a clipping breeze and smooth water on this inland lake.

The run from Hamburg up the Alster Lake was most exciting work, owing to the sudden sharp puffs and the number of boats and steamers dodging about. Every spar and portion of gear were severely tested by the puffs, as it was a case of "crack on," and being the end of the voyage, spars or gear might be carried away without much inconvenience arising.

The mouth of the river is very narrow, and little steamers ply about a mile up it. I had got half a mile in, when a furious gust came just at the moment that I lowered the sliding gunter, the boom jibbed over and knocked my hat overboard.

By the time that I had topped the boom and got

the jib in, the hat was some distance astern, and the steamer, which I knew was due, was not far off. There seemed just time to paddle back and pick up the hat before the boat should run it down. I reached the hat, seized it, and turned the canoe. I had only given two strokes ahead when the steamer came gliding along, with a sort of compressed breathing noise, carrying with her a little mountain of water on each side, as she all but filled up the width of the whole river. There was no time to land, so I awaited the ducking, which seemed inevitable. Luckily the wave came so fast that, instead of the canoe's stern rising to it and broaching-to on the crest, it buried itself deeply in, and the mackintosh apron and arched cedar deck caused the water to pass harmlessly along.

It was blowing very stiff, so the boat got over a large space in a short time.

Several small rapids had to be waded, the canoe sailing up them beautifully by herself. At the head of each I regained my seat and was pleasantly whirled along zigzags, round sharp bends, requiring constant shifting of the boom and most cute steering. When luncheon-time arrived, somehow all the best luncheon places had been passed: it always is so: the saying on board was "just a little further; and round the next reach there is sure to be a quiet shady spot;" thus it went on for a mile or two; at last *the* spot was found and luncheon soon spread and ditto vanished; sails were then stowed away and everything made snug for the downward passage.

The current carried me swiftly back, past all the pretty scenes of the morning, only that each came into view from a different point, as I was now descending the stream; the lake was soon reached, mast stepped, main and jib set, and a pleasant "beat" back to Hamburg finished a most enjoyable day.

Next day, the breeze having increased to a gale during the night, there was quite a lively set of seas on the Alster Lake; a sailing cruise there was the order of the day.

There were several yachts out, and all had reefs in; so, on starting, being under the lee of the houses, I took one reef in as a precaution. One reef was enough for running before the wind, but when bringing her round to the wind she required another reef down: this was done "in stays" and the points tied on the next tack. Amongst the yachts out, one attracted my attention especially, on account of the reckless amount of canvas she was carrying when running; she had the wind on her port quarter, and the three men in her were all sitting up as far as possible to windward and aft, yet she had her head completely under water, ploughing it up in a very "swamping-like" manner.

Shortly after I had landed, to lunch at a friend's house,

on looking back across the lake, there she was, or rather there was her masthead alone visible ; she having capsized and sunk on being brought "to the wind ;" the men had just been landed all right.

After luncheon I sailed across to inspect the wreck more closely ; several boats were made fast to her, and she was being dragged slowly along the bottom towards the shore.

It was then blowing very hard, and the boatmen had great difficulty in getting their tow-ropes made fast to the mast, owing to the sharp seas that threatened to swamp them.

CHAPTER XX.

"PUT THAT SAIL DOWN"—GREEN LIGHTS—STREET CANALS.

I HAD some bladders full of water stowed along the bottom of the canoe, to act as ballast, water being safer than stone ballast, as in the event of capsizing, water of course loses its weight. Sailing in these short lively seas was very wet work. As I was only cruising about for pleasure, I had shaken out a reef, and it soon became evident that she had a little too much sail on her: so I intended to take the close reef in on her next tack. I had just "gone about" near the shore and was preparing to reef, when I heard a man shouting imperatively in English, from between his two hands, "Put that sail down!" At first I took no notice, but he reiterated his command in so authoritative a manner, that I put her about again and stood back to find out what he wanted. On nearing the shore, where he was standing with others, I saw a small inlet running under a bridge, with a quiet pool beyond; so I steered through and pulled up alongside the bank. Here this "Nautical Instructor" stoutly demanded, "Why did you not take that sail down?" It was doubtless kindly meant; so I answered, that I was about to take in a reef for my own convenience—that might also, perhaps, please him. Not a bit; he then wanted to know whether I was not mad, "to go on the water in such a little boat when even a big cutter had just been swamped."

As soon as the reef was in and the boat once more close hauled to the breeze, he seemed satisfied, as she was going slower and drier over the water; but a puff coming on caused him to shout again to me as vigorously as before.

Night cruising on the town end of the lake, was very pleasant but very dangerous, owing to the number of boats steaming and pulling about in all directions.

One night, when returning late from our friend's house on the outer lake, I had a very narrow escape of being cut in two: the night was pitch dark and boats' lights in all directions; a stiff breeze and pelting rain rendered hearing out of the question; after paddling about a mile, I noticed a small *green light* on my port beam, and knew that it should be a vessel going on a course parallel to my own; when, judge my surprise, I saw it growing larger and then coming straight at me in short bounds. I gave a loud yell and a quick stroke ahead, and then a

A CLIPPING BREEZE.

heavy splash back, sending a shower of water over the three or four foremost rowers, which caused them to stop and unship their oars, which, on the next stroke, would have hit my back or gone through the deck of the canoe. I then found it was a twelve-oared club boat with a single green light in the bows. Now, according to the international "rule of the road," all open boats are to carry a *single white light*, and sailing vessels *red* and *green* sidelights; steamers, red and green side-lights as well as a white mast-head light.

This boat kept a very bad "look-out." They ran foul of a boat at anchor a minute or two after our meeting, and probably had never noticed my white light on the mast; though it was so fixed that the motion of the boat caused by paddling would swing it round the mast on one stroke, and back again on the next stroke, rendering it visible nearly all round.

Having stayed a week in Hamburg, the end of our cruising time approached, and after one more delightful run with a clipping breeze, the canoes were taken to a large warehouse, from which they were to be sent by lighter to the steamer *Berlin*, in which we intended to take our passage to London.

Next day, finding that the *Berlin* was moored in the Elbe, off Altona, I went to the warehouse, to ascertain whether the boats had started. I found them still there, and as it was a long way to go down the Elbe, I feared we might lose our passage, for it was nearly low water in the canal, and no lighter ready; so at once I slung my canoe by its painter, hooked on the crane-rope, and got the men to lower the boat and her skipper together into the muddy street-canal below the warehouse.

CHAPTER XXI.

WATER LABYRINTH—CLOSE SHAVE IN A LOCK—THE ELBE AT LAST—THE "BERLIN"—STARTING FOR LONDON—THE THAMES.

ALL the neighbouring windows were soon crowded, and on inquiring of the warehousemen which was the shortest way to the Elbe, as many voices from the different windows screamed out in favour of this way as of that. Twenty or thirty hands pointed, some to the right, others to the left; hot arguments ensued amongst them, all equally anxious to prove themselves correct, shouting and swearing at one another across the water-lane.

I simply took the direction towards which the bow happened to point, to save the trouble of turning in a muddy course scarcely wider than the boat's length. Having worked my way from one end to the other of various tortuous water lanes, where the gaunt old houses leaned over, nearly meeting at the top, I came upon a dingy black lock-gate, some twenty feet high, with equally high slimy walls on both sides, and a few old wooden worm-eaten piles standing out two or three feet from them as a protection against bumps from barges. As I neared their gates, they opened, and a minute screw-steamer towed three lumbering barges out. I dodged between the old piles and the wall, to await their passing; and before this was over, from another canal, which branched in here, arrived another tug with three more barges, all of which entered the lock. I leaped on board the final barge, and hauled my canoe on board after me, just as the lock-gates closed a foot or two behind her stern. Then I watched to see whether the water would rise or lower, and was satisfied to find that it was lowering.

Then, for the first time, I knew that I was on the right track, as the Elbe is lower than the other waters in Hamburg. The opposite lock-gates opened, the barges were towed out, and I again launched my canoe, but this time on the Elbe itself. After paddling some distance among ships and small craft, under warps and chains, round floating timber and great clumsy buoys, I entered the mid stream. Here the fresh westerly wind was against a strong ebb tide, and, consequently, my paddle down to Altona was a very wet one. Having reached the steamer the canoe was soon hauled into the lighter alongside, thence handed up into the starboard quarter-boat of the

Berlin, and safely lashed, as a very rough passage was anticipated.

There I left her, and, with mind at ease, threaded my way back to the *Kronprinz*; and at 10 P.M., H. and I drove down to the Altona landing-place to embark.

A busy scene it was,—great was the rush and violent the tumult. Alongside the pier was a cattle-steamer, blowing off steam and shipping oxen in a hurry. Outside that was the *Berlin*, compelled thus to drag her sheep and passengers across the labyrinth of heterogeneous litter, both living and inanimate, which cumbered the deck of the cattle-boat. Lights, planks, ropes, men and masters, animals, shouts, baas, and steam were gloriously intermingled, diverting, though only for a time, one's attention from the gale, rain, and lightning.

Presently, one by one, the ordinary lights were extinguished, giving place to green and red lights, and to the brighter mast-head lamp. Steam was shut up for use; passengers turned in below; sheep were quiet, with the exception of one or two moaning baas; the jacks put on their oilskins and took their places; our captain mounted the bridge: "Let go of all" ("*Ezee a ead*"), and the *Berlin* was under weigh.

Outside, the weather was very bad; the engines had to be eased, on account of the heavy seas over and through which we were plunging; but it was just the style of journey to suit the steward, as nearly all the passengers had contracted for food for the whole term of the voyage, yet few indeed could even bear the sight of meals, much less attempt to eat.

I had heard that the North Sea was capable of being lashed into fury by a westerly gale: certainly the sight was as grand as any I have witnessed in the Atlantic.

For two days I enjoyed the steamer's bridge; then we peacefully entered the Thames, the passengers reappeared on deck, the busy hives of London swarmed around us; the Custom-house officers passed the *Nautilus*, and the *Nautilus* passed the Custom-house on the last of the flood tide to Westminster Bridge, where two men out of the crowd, even there collected, lodged her once more, safely, amongst her sisters at Searle's. Rather scratched and bumped, well-seasoned with brine and sun, but still sound in wind and limb, the *Nautilus* was left to be overhauled preparatory to a cruise in the Mediterranean.

PART II.

PRACTICAL HINTS ON BUILDING AND FITTING CANOES.

CHAPTER XXII.

NAUTILUS NO. I—DEFECTS—DIVING—SINKING—NO CABIN.

PERFECTION in canoe travelling is still a long way ahead, even as yet out of sight. The fair wind which we want is *improvement;* and the only course, *experiment*, must be beaten on "both tacks"—theory and practice, against ignorance and prejudice.

Improvement in all departments, man, boat, and stores, is necessary. A man soon improves himself by gaining experience, with which he improves his canoe and its internal arrangements, gear, fittings, and stores. A cruise, however short, seldom passes without giving some new experience or suggesting some new dodge, which will be improved, cancelled, or stuck to in the next, and always gives "practice" (which, according to copy-books, "makes perfect"). A canoeist, to enjoy thoroughly a cruise in foreign waters, should possess as many as he possibly can of the following qualities :—

A strong body and mind, presence of mind especially; a love for the water; the power of swimming (with his clothes on); smartness in cruising, bivouacking, fishing, shooting (rapids and birds); the faculty of making himself understood; a perfect canoe, sails, fittings, and stores.

The plan of a perfect cruising canoe can only be arrived at by mustering together theoretical and practical knowledge, and making experiments with plans and models.

In these plans, the shape, size, use, and weight of each piece of wood used in the construction of the boat must be considered in connection with the different qualities required in a travelling canoe.

Sailing powers—in bad as well as fine weather; a good shear; water-tight compartments and water ballast, making her a life-boat.

Sails—that can be set, reefed, and taken in without moving from one's seat.

Strength—to bear lifting at all parts, bumping on rocks, and sleeping ashore in her.

Weight—as light as consistent with strength, for transporting over land; light draught of water for shallows and paddling.

I built my first canoe at Bonchurch, Isle of Wight, in 1866. Her length was only 9 feet; beam, 2 feet 6 inches; and depth about 9 inches; clincher built of fir, and canvas decked. On launching, it was found she could not support my weight, so she was opened aft; and a semicircular bulkhead let in, which did not add to her good looks, making her like a Dutch "billy-boy's" dingy. Her seagoing qualities far exceeded anticipation; and, though often rolled over in the surf, and bumped on the rocks, she is still in existence at Newport.

The *Nautilus* No. 1 (used in Sweden and the Baltic) was built by Searle and Sons, Lambeth, of the same dimensions as the *Rob Roy*, No. 2, namely—length, 14 feet; beam, 26 inches; 6 inches abaft midships; total depth, 1 foot; camber, 1 inch; depth at gunwale, $8\frac{1}{2}$ inches; well, 32 inches long by 20 inches broad; paddle, 7 feet. Sliding gunter rigged. Built of oak, with cedar deck and mahogany topstreak. The tops of her stem and stern posts were lower than the deck line at midships, which made running (with sails) dangerous when the water was lumpy. As the swell caught her up she felt the breeze more, and, gaining "way," would overrun the sea in a downward direction, bury her bows under water, and "lose her way," when the following sea, powerfully lifting her under the quarters, would either swamp or capsize her. Therefore, a fresh fair wind during her cruises in the Swedish lakes, Mediterranean Sea, and the Solent, was considered as bad as a head-wind. Sleeping in her, as may be seen in the first night of the log, was very uncomfortable. Standing up when "under way" was always a ticklish job; but her worst quality was her diving propensity, which not only made her uncomfortable, but sadly interfered with the pleasure of carrying a press of sail.

A boat with so many and glaring defects was certainly not worth keeping: I therefore designed a new one, endeavouring to obviate these several faults.

The great drawbacks of *Nautilus* No. 1, were:—

(1.) Diving when running. The remedy, good shear and camber.

(2.) Sinking if swamped; requiring, therefore, two water-tight compartments, one at each end, sufficient to support man and stores if the middle compartment got full of water.

(3.) Bad cabin accommodation; therefore breadth, depth, length, and open space were required amidships for the owner to lie at full length and be able to turn with ease. Good beam, with flat floor, would insure better sailing qualities, and facilitate standing up and moving about whilst afloat—points of special moment when boarding or leaving steamers, or yachts "under way."

I placed my plans in the hands of Messenger, boat-builder at Teddington; and being the first canoe with such a "kink," it was rather a puzzle to build.

CHAPTER XXIII.

NAUTILUS NO. 2—DIMENSIONS—RIGS—LIFE-BOAT QUALITIES.

HER *length* was 14 feet; *beam* at bottom of topstreak, 2 feet 4 inches; 6 inches abaft midships; *depth* from top of topstreak at midships to bottom of keel, 1 foot 1 inch; *depth* from top of stem-post to ground, 1 foot 9 inches; top of stern-post to ground, 1 foot 6 inches. *Draught* of water, 5 inches. The hatchway octagon-shaped: total length, including locker, 4 feet 5 inches; breadth of side parallel, 1 foot 9 inches; fore and after ends, 1 foot; depth of combing, 1½ inch. Sleeping space between the water-tight bulkheads, 5 feet 9 inches. The locker bulkhead can be lifted out for sleeping.

Many kinds of rigging have been used, but only the two best retained for work: they are sliding gunter and standing lug.

Sliding gunter mainsail is—foot, 5 feet 9 inches; after

leach, 9 feet. Luff, 8 feet, of which 5 feet is laced to the gaff. Jib—luff, 5 feet 6 inches; foot, 4 feet; leach, 3 feet 8 inches. Dandy—luff, 3 feet 10 inches; leach, 4 feet 4 inches; foot, 2 feet 9 inches.

Lug rig mainsail—foot, 5 feet 8 inches; after leach, 9 feet; luff, 4 feet 5 inches; head, 5 feet 8 inches. Jib—luff, 5 feet 6 inches; leach, 3 feet 8 inches; foot, 4 feet. Dandy, same as for sliding gunter.

The mainmast is stepped 4 feet 6 inches from stem-post, and dandy (spare gaff with storm mainsail) 3 feet 6 inches from stern post, in a tube, as it steps in air compartment. The paddle is 7 feet long, $6\frac{1}{2}$ inches flat blades, used, when sailing, in a crutch in the lee gunwale.

A half hatch and apron cover the well in bad weather, but in moderate weather the apron is stowed below: the half-hatch, having a loop-rack, is used for stowing the coils of halliards, topping lifts, &c., thus keeping the well all clear. This boat sails well with a fresh breeze on her beam, and will "stay" in smooth water. Her running qualities were proved to be first-rate by many a run from Ryde to Portsmouth in strong breezes, which, when against tide, made as nasty a slop as any man could wish for in which to test the seagoing powers of his canoe; as the large seas of an open seaway are not half so dangerous as those of a tide race. I also made experiments in her self-righting qualities by paddling out on the Solent and then capsizing her: out of three experiments she righted herself twice, and each time I was able to get in again over the stern. The third time, she "hung fire," and I had only to give her a touch, as I swam, when she at once righted. I then filled the middle compartment with water and got in again from swimming, and found her even then quite manageable. Afterwards I took in two large stones, about ten or fifteen pounds each (the water still inside), they made her sink within two inches of the deck at midships, but still she floated, and I was able to bale her out, and afterwards to change my clothes with ease, whilst afloat, leaving in the distance the small mob which had collected on the beach whilst the masonry was being shipped and tried.

After carefully watching and trying all her points, I think her design might be slightly altered for the better. The theoretical outline has been proved correct, and now lightness and strength must combine with compactness, and beauty mingle with the whole.

The following design is only calculated to fit the author, and as a safe and comfortable travelling boat, chiefly for lake and sea work. If river cruising were the chief object, extra length and less keel would be allowed; or if for a heavier man, extra length. Only general outlines are here given, the minutiæ must be filled in according to the taste of each owner. 14 feet 6 inches was decided at the canoe club on December 19th, as the extreme length for oak canoes, eligible for the twelve-miles' race; this should be borne in mind by men who intend to enter for these races.

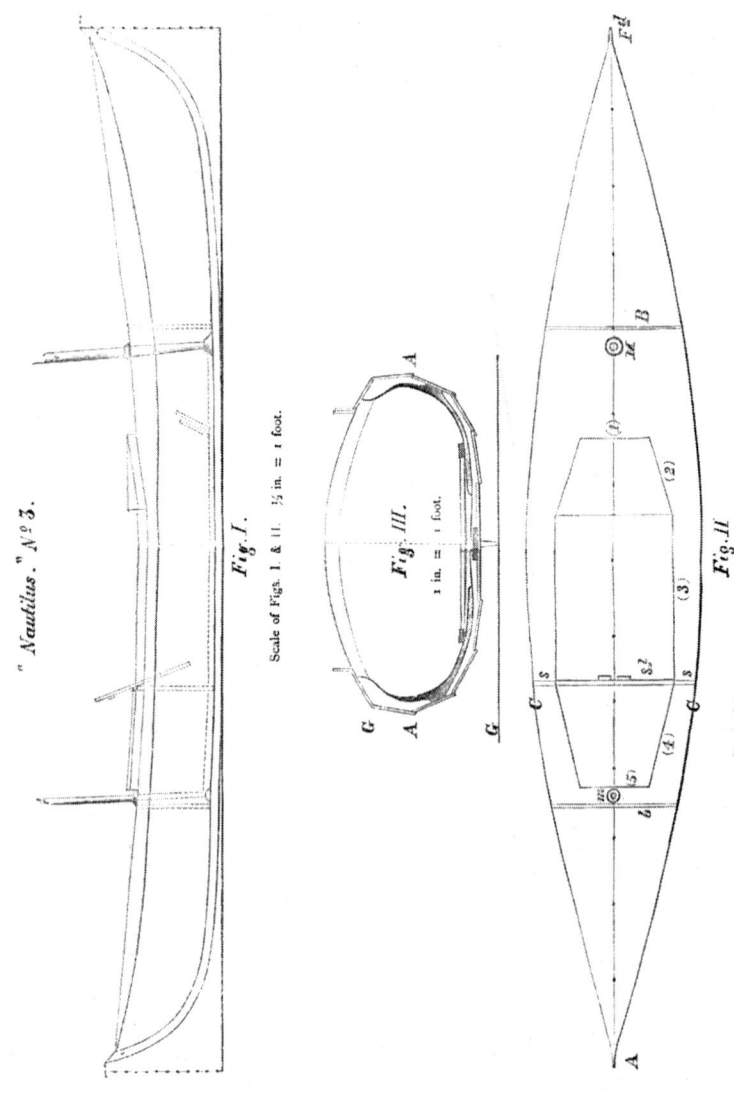

"Nautilus." N.º 3.

Fig. I.

Scale of Figs. I & II. ½ in. = 1 foot.

Fig. III.
1 in. = 1 foot.

Fig. II.

CHAPTER XXIV.

NAUTILUS NO. 3—DIMENSIONS—BULKHEADS, ETC.

THE dimensions of the following design have been carefully selected and compiled in the hope of producing a canoe, many steps nearer perfection than the last; every point has been well considered with relation to the size and weight of the owner, and the purpose for which she is intended to be used, namely travelling. She is therefore designed to fit a man (whose weight is 11 stone 10 pounds; height, 5 feet 8 inches, length of leg from hip, 3 feet 7 inches; breadth of shoulders, 1 foot 10 inches; and stern, 1 foot 4 inches) and his baggage and dog. The dimensions of the canoe are, *Length, fig.* 1, from top of stem to top of stern post, 14 feet; *Depth*, at midships from top of "topstreak" to bottom of keel, $10\frac{1}{4}$ inches; height of stem post above the level of keel, 1 foot $10\frac{1}{4}$ inches; height of stern post, ditto, 1 foot $7\frac{1}{2}$ inches; camber, 2 inches; depth of keel, $1\frac{1}{2}$ inches.

Deck plan, fig. 2. Beam amidships at bottom of topstreak, 2 feet 4 inches; beam at mast-hole, 2 feet; beam at dandy, 1 foot 8 inches. The greatest beam is amidships, not at seat, anticipating water ballast and stores, stowed forward when cruising abroad, but in light river work at home when these are not required, the baggage can be stowed forward, and the wheels and dog in the locker; in this way, with the additional weight of mast and gear standing forward, the canoe floats on an "even keel." Also, all pressure of wind on the head sails tends to put her "down by the head."

The water-tight bulkheads B b (*fig.* 2) are placed B 4 feet from F^a (forward) and b, 3 feet 5 inches from A, enclosing sufficient air to support the canoe and owner when the remaining compartment is full of water. The mainmast M is stepped 4 feet 3 inches from F; only very slight rake is given, so that the sliding-gunter or lug rig can be used. The mizen or dandy m is 3 feet 7 inches from A. The hatchway is octangular shape, (1) = 1 foot, (2) = 1 foot 1 inch, (3) = 2 feet 5 inches, (4) = 1 foot 5 inches, (5) = 1 foot, depth of combing, 1½ inches. The locker is formed by a sliding bulkhead (S^1) with two standing sides (s); the backboard rests on the top of this bulkhead, and a space is cut on the port side to admit the ends of the spars when stowed below, the locker being finally enclosed by a flat lid, hinged to the after combing, and secured from opening when capsized by a pin through the bulkhead into the lid.

The stretcher is placed 3 feet 10 inches from the top of the sliding bulkhead; being very low in the centre, it allows the sails stowage room and at the same time acts as a moveable bulkhead, preventing the derangement of stores and ballast when "hauling over" obstacles or when capsized; this plan appears to me the best for a stretcher; the sideboard plan is as comfortable for the feet, but does not prevent the baggage falling aft when lifted "stem up," nor does it prevent its floating out when swamped; the sliding stretcher is used by some canoeists, but to me it seems more troublesome than useful.

In *fig.* 3, plate 1, the greatest beam, A to H, is 2 feet 4 inches. Depth from gunwale to ground $gg = 10\frac{1}{2}$ inches; depth inside from deck to kelson = 1 foot, topstreak (cedar) = $3\frac{1}{2}$ inches deep, oak planks, 4 inches deep, oak keel, $1\frac{1}{2}$ inches, cedar or birch beam at ends of hatch, $1\frac{1}{2}$ inches deep, combing cedar, $1\frac{1}{2}$ inches deep. Floor boards, total width, 1 foot 4 inches, length 4 feet 8 inches. Oak knees support to deck at sides of well. Timbers are made of oak, birch, or ash; those placed near the seat should be 6 inches apart, others 1 foot and 1 foot and a half.

The mainmast should be stepped in a tube $1\frac{3}{4}$ inches diameter from deck to oak step on kelson; this must be strongly fitted, as a great strain is put on it when carrying a press of sail. The reason for stepping the mast in a tube is, that with no tube, in the event of being capsized, if the mast only came half out, the canoe would try to right herself, and the heave of the sea and body of water in the belly of the sail, would probably rip the deck up, using the mast as a crowbar. The large amount of shear is given for many reasons, the two principal of which are to prevent diving when running before short seas, and to create a tendency to right herself after being capsized.

In perfectly calm water, having carefully turned the canoe bottom up, she might float in that position, but the least touch or ripple would start her righting powers, and with any "lop" or sea on, it would be impossible for her to float "bottom up" of her own accord, provided the masts and sails are unshipped.

CHAPTER XXV.

BUILDING—WOOD—WEIGHTS OF WOOD, ETC.

BEFORE the actual building is commenced, a careful plan should be made, in which all the different requirements of a thorough travelling canoe (namely, seagoing, sailing, lifeboat, sleeping, and land transporting qualities) have been considered; the minutiæ changed, twisted, and experimented on until all the bad points have been cancelled and the good ones fitted in the most ship-shape manner.

The next point to be considered is the wood, to select only such as will stand the wear and tear of travelling, the bumps on rocks, the weight of one's body when sleeping in her on shore, a scorching sun, a snag in the water, jolting in carts, railways, and steamers.

English oak I have found best.

Cedar, though a very light and nice-looking wood, is very apt to split when exposed to a hot sun. To sleep in a cedar canoe without cracking the planks or timbers, requires a soft bed for the canoe itself, and a light, quiet sleeping owner inside.

Red pine is a very hard, heavy, and ugly wood, therefore seldom used in light boats; it is very strong, and will stand hard work, provided the planks have been well chosen as to grain and knots.

Yellow pine is very light, but also very weak: it is much used in the construction of up-river boats, required only for light work and smooth water; it makes better spars for canoeing than any other wood. Straight, close grain and no knots being a *sine quâ non*, well-chosen spars of this wood stand stiffer and are lighter than others. One of the advantages of this wood is that the spar will break before any part of the deck round it, on coming in contact suddenly and forcibly with a bridge, rope, or branch of a tree, when oak or ash would bend and finally carry away the surrounding deck. In a wild country a spar can nearly always be replaced, but mending the deck would be a much more difficult job.*

Birch.—This wood is very useful for making tough

---

* Pine masts were used even by the ancient Greeks, at the time of the Trojan war; and shortly after, in Homer's *Od.* ii. 424, we are told: Telemachus and Athena start on a cruise in search of Ulysses; the goddess causing a fair wind to spring up, Telemachus gave the orders to lay the oars in and make sail. "Raising up the *pine* mast (ἱστὸν ἐλάτινον), they stepped it through the centre cross-plank" (thwart).

beams, timbers, or carlines: it might do for the axletree of the wheels, used in land transport.

Box-wood.—All the blocks should be of box-wood with brass sheaves (wooden ones are apt to swell and jam when exposed to wet weather).

Ash.—The only spar which ought to be at all heavy and bendable is the boom; an *ash* boom will be found to keep the sail better set in light weather than a yellow pine one, and in squally weather will bend to the puffs, and thus modify the sudden strain in the sail; the boat-hook also should be of ash.

The relative weights of these woods in pieces of the same size, are:

Oak	12 lbs.
Yellow Deal	11 ,,
Cedar	7 ,,
Mahogany	10 ,,

Therefore an oak boat is five-twelfths heavier than one built of cedar.

For rough work, *oak* is undoubtedly the best, and as a canoe may at any moment, during a cruise, have to stand hard knocks and wrenches, I think a better wood than oak, for her bottom, keel, and sides, cannot be found. The keel piece must be perfectly straight grained. The stem and stern posts in some oak-bottomed canoes are made of mahogany, but it appears to me that the few ounces less weight thus saved cannot compensate for the loss of strength at these most vulnerable parts; therefore I have oak. The three floor planks on each side of the kelson should be strong, but the fourth light, as it is not so exposed to bumps. The topstreak is usually of cedar or mahogany, which answers well; the timbers may be of oak, ash, or birch. Cedar is by far the best wood for the decks, but must be well selected, avoiding cracks, and carefully fitted and rounded; a good plan is to have some fore and aft carlines let into the tops of the beams, this makes the deck strong enough to stand or sit on, yet adds very little weight to the whole.

CHAPTER XXVI.

RIGS :— LATEEN, SETTEE, CHINESE — DIPPING LUG — REVOLVING LUG—STANDING LUG—SPREET SAIL—SLIDING GUNTER—SLIDING SPREET—DANDY—FORE-SAILS.

"RIGS for boats" have always been the subject of the hottest arguments amongst yachtmen, sailing boatmen, and canoeists. Each "skipper" backs his own boat's rig, and very rightly too, if he thinks it the best; but the "cause of rigs" is seldom promoted by these pen skirmishes; the aim being too often not so much to prove the good points of their own, as to try to cut up the rig of others.

Few men have time or care to tinker their boats about, to try all the numerous kinds of rigs, so as to arrive at any real conclusion as to which is the best in all points.

Many rigs are called *failures*, because they did not answer on *the one* occasion of their trial. A rig, to be fairly tried, must not only be shifted about in the boat itself, but also tried in different states of weather and sea ; and, if possible, in company with other boats, so as to test the speed and weatherly qualities.

Having closely watched the movements, and sailed in the boats of the Cornish fishermen, Portsmouth wherries, ships' cutters and gigs; the boats of the Portuguese, Spanish, Maltese, Egyptians, Mediterranean-French, South Africans, and East Indians; and seen the Swedish, Danish, German, and China rigged boats working, I have, after considering the qualities of each in relation to English-shaped boats and canoes, tried in various ways and weather, the three which seemed most adapted to them, namely, standing lug, spreet sail, and sliding gunter, with jib or dandy, or both, as no boat should be rigged with only one sail (except a centre-board or a revolver).

It may be well to take a passing glance at those rigs least adaptable to canoes, before considering those which have been tried and fitted, bearing in mind the chief points required in a canoe's sails, lightness and low body, easy to be set, taken in, and stowed below.

Lateen Rig.—This rig is used by the Portuguese, Spanish, Egyptians, and in fact everywhere in the Mediterranean. The boats are generally fitted with two lateens and a balloon jib for light weather; most of them are coasters of from ten to fifty tons, and usually full decked and well manned; the sails are reefed on the head, and the joints tied round the yard aloft, by men and boys, as the yard is seldom if ever lowered.

The small open pleasure and fishing boats of Marseilles are rigged with one lateen, and jib forward, and a dandy aft; the boatmen do somehow manage to work the sail, but the long yard is a very awkward thing to handle when reefing in a sea way.

The lateen, as a canoe sail, is one of the most elegant, and at the same time dangerous sails she could attempt to carry. The yard would be as long as the canoe (it might be jointed, with a ferrule to connect it), and as the sail reefs on the yard, it would be a difficult operation in a strong breeze to work at either end in making the reef fast. Its good points are the short mast, and that the sail makes a good tent; the great spread of sail would "pay well" in very light breezes, but, for travelling, paddling would pay better.

Settee rig is chiefly used by the East Indians in their long sharp river boats; the sail nearly the same shape as the lateen, the difference being, that the fore-corner is cut off and the yard not so long aft, forming, in fact, an exaggerated dipping lug.

The mast for these sails, in the country boats, generally rakes forward. As a canoe sail, it is very good for those river-going canoes which are not likely to do much sea or large lake work; its great advantages being its very short mast and large spread of sail, so that on coming to one of those low bridges one often meets with on unnavigated rivers, by simply letting go the halliards, she can pass under, the mast being only as high as the captain's head. The high peak also gets many a puff from over the bank-top, which would seldom fill a low sail.

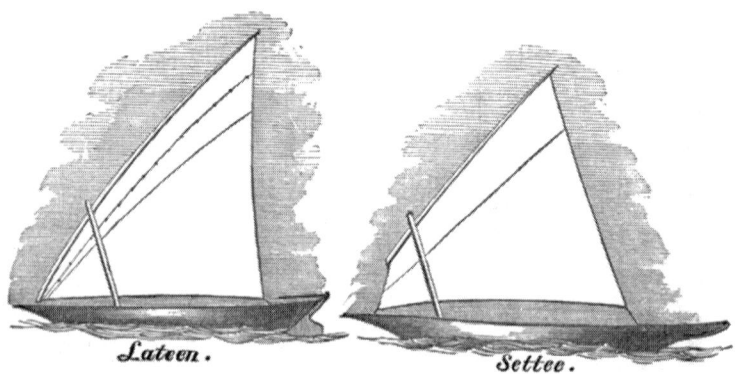

Lateen.   Settee.

As a seagoing sail it is nearly useless: the length of yard, the difficulty of hooking the tack, and the want of a boom being serious objections, where a man has to do all the work from his sitting posture.

The Chinese rig is a very snug one; sails thus fitted set flat, and, when the halliards are let go for shortening sail, the sail comes down snug by the mast. The mast for these sails must be lofty, which, though not convenient in a canoe, may be borne with for the sake of a good sail.

Either one or two sails might be used: a large one forward, no jib, and a small mizen aft, would make a nice working rig. About one quarter of the boom and one quarter of the yard should project forward of the mast, and the bamboo stretchers which cross the sail should be hooped or parallel to the mast.

Chinese Rig.

The Chinese use several sheets, one from each of the lower battens, which are "tailed off" into one long end for belaying on deck; but for a canoe one sheet is enough. A topping lift, fitted as a brail, is required to ensure snug stowage of the sail when down; it can be fitted thus: one end is made fast at the mast-head, and the other is then rove through a cringle on the boom, about one-third from after end, carried up the other side of the sail, goes through a block at the mast-head, leading thence on deck. For a reef, lower till the first batten is on the boom, let the sheet go and the sail will point its fore part in an aft direction, hook the tack cringle, haul in the sheet, hook the after cringle, and the reef is in; as the batten acts instead of points in keeping a flat foot (one or two points might be handy in keeping the slack sail up).

Dipping lugs are used by the Cornish fishing boats, man-of-war gigs and cutters, the boatmen of East Indian ports, Egyptians, and many others. There is no boom, the tack has to be hauled down in the bows of the boat, and the sail has to be shifted to the other side of the mast on going about; these are decided faults when looking at them from a canoe point of view. Going about is practised in two different ways; the English plan is to lower the sail when the wind comes on the bow of the new tack and the sail has backed her round, unhook the yard and tack, pass abaft to the other side of the mast, hook on yard and tack, hoist away.

The Egyptians never "go about" but "wear round." On coming to the end of a tack, they put the helm hard up (right across her stern): this deadens her way; when she brings the wind right aft, then they pass the sheet round before the leach of the sail and bring it aft the other side, and the wind lifts the body of the sail over the yard and mast-head, the yard being chock up and no mast above the sheave hole, the sheet is hauled aft, and the new board sailed with the yard loft one side and the sail on the other side of the mast.

Revolving lug.—The lug may be fitted in somewhat the same manner as the Chinese principle (but without the sail stretchers and mast hoops), that is, with a portion of both yard and boom projecting forward of the mast; the boom should be toggled, $\frac{1}{4}$ its length from the fore end to the mast at sufficient height from the deck to allow clear play when swinging about; the yard is then slung and hoisted in the usual way, with mast-traveller, and when well up the sail sets as flat as a board. If sufficient length to toggle, and distance between traveller and sheave have been allowed, the sail can be worked like a weathercock. In a hard squall let go the sheet, retaining the bare end, and the sail flies round till its luff points in the "wind's eye."

The sail being set so flat will not bang about like most sails, which then need to be lowered to save the mast. Reefing this sail requires the untoggling of the boom to get at the tack cringles. The sail should always be laced to the boom, and when a mizen is used the main should be stepped well forward; no jib is required.

Standing lug.—The safety, beauty, and handiness of this rig entirely depend on the cut and fittings of the sail. For safety the yard should be hooked to a traveller on the mast, which will work quickly, and the reefing department should be as simple as possible, so that you can "lower away," hook the tack and after leach cringles, "hoist away" and then tie the points at leisure. For this mode of reefing have one hook at the tack end of the boom, and one or two, according to the number of reefs, at the after end at the right distances for the cringles. The dimensions

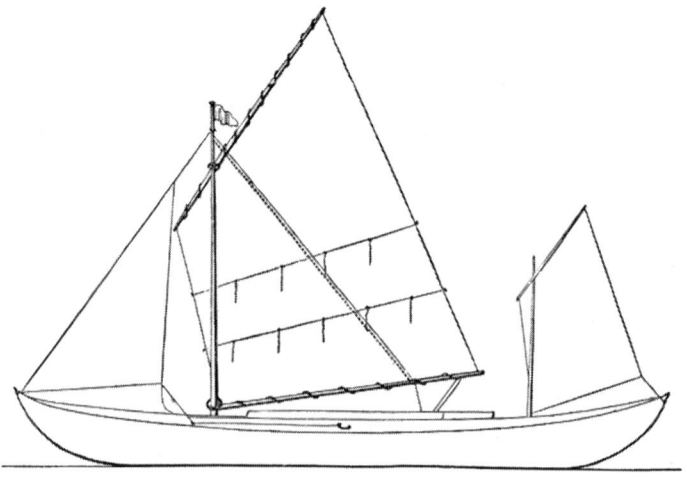

STANDING LUG AND MIZEN.

of my rig are :—mast-head to deck 7 feet, boom 6 feet, yard 6 feet, sail leach 9 feet, foot 6 feet, head 6 feet, luff 4 feet 5 inches.

For cruising this sail can be fitted with a double topping

lift, which is very useful in shortening sail smartly, as it gathers the sail up and prevents the boom getting into the water; it should be rove at the mast-head through the eyes of a grummet (which can be lifted off the mast-head by the boat-hook); when the boom is in sailing position the two parts of the lift should meet and splice on the fore side of the grummet, then lead to deck and aft in a single part, or, one end may be made fast aloft.

The luff should be strongly roped, as the constant strain is apt to stretch it, and therefore spoils the set of the sail.

The blot of this rig is the lofty mast required, and smallness of its jib, the yard projecting forward needing clear swinging room.

A gaff topsail may be used with this rig, but as it would only do in very light fair winds, for travelling paddling would be found better.

Spreet sails are used chiefly in small open boats: the only large vessels I have seen *spreet rigged* are the Thames sailing barges. The Swedish open boats, met with during the cruise, were nearly all spreet rigged, but the sail was a very ugly shape; the peak of the sail was only the same height as the throat, the whole sail forming a square. The Portsmouth wherries are amongst the fastest and handiest open boats of England: they are mostly yawl rigged, with spreet sails; their sails are of the lofty narrow class, the main and mizen being each nearly the same width at the throat as the foot; the fore-sail is also lofty and narrow, but each sail sets as "flat as a board." The weatherly quality of this rig is greatly augmented by the deep keel, sharp bow, and clean run of these boats; nevertheless, on any boat these sails stand the same, and, if properly balancing each other, the boat will be found easier to handle than if rigged with lugs, settee or gaffs (as some ship's boats are). I have often sailed ship's cutters, and lifeboats yawl-rigged with spreet sails, but the difficulty always was, to get the mizen so placed as to require no jib. The wherries always carry their mizens *inboard*, whereas ship-cutters and lifeboats generally are sent from the builders with the mizen fittings placed for the sail to set *out over* the stern, in which position it must have a jib as well as foresail to balance it. Though the spreet is a good rig for boats, it would be just the opposite for canoes, owing to the numerous *standing* fittings required; the luff of the sail has to be ringed or laced to a lofty mast, therefore cannot be quickly unshipped and stowed below; also a long spreet is required.

The usual method of shortening sail with this rig is, by brailing up: therefore the whole hoist of the sail remains with goodly bunches of sail and gear for the squall to play with, which would not be either safe or pleasant in a light canoe.

The head of the sail is its best point, however close reefed, the good head always remains. The sailing barges of the Thames are rigged with spreet sail, foresail, and spreet mizen: they work remarkably well, and as their proportions and masting resemble those of a canoe to a great extent, it may be well to take a glance at them. The barge carries her mainsail and foresail well forward, allowing cargo space amidships; so does the canoe, she allowing space for the owner to sit in: but the barge always carries a mizen aft, to balance the sails forward:

SPREET-RIGGED WHERRY.

now this a canoe does not always do, as at least two-thirds of those afloat carry no after sail, which accounts for the paddle being so often seen on the wrong side of the boat when sailing on a wind. The barge also carries a leeboard, a *sine quâ non* for all flat-bottomed vessels of light draft, which desire to turn to windward. The barge has the advantage from her size, as her man on deck does not comparatively show much front to the wind, whereas in the canoe the captain's body confronts the wind to a detrimental extent. A yawl yacht, with a square haystack on her quarterdeck, would make poor tracks when beating to windward.

Sliding gunter.—After trying various rigs before going to Sweden, the sliding gunter proved the handiest; though, from its high pointed peak, it did not hold quite so good a wind as a square-headed lug. The fault is on the safe side in rough and squally weather, but various alterations and improvements had to be made to adapt it to a canoe. These were accomplished before starting, and since then the only faults have been in the cutting and sewing the sail itself. These sails require most delicate lining, cutting, and sewing, so as not to stretch any part. As the selvage must be the after leach, therefore the whole luff is bias and will stretch at the shadow of the word, and if it be stretched one inch, the after leach will never stand well.

The sail is made in one piece, and roped only on the luff and foot; two reefs; and eyelet holes for boom and gaff lacing.

The gaff in the ordinary rig is kept to the mast by iron rings fastened to its heel, about a quarter the length of the gaff, apart, which travel up and down the mast; but

GUNTER-BRASS.

as this prohibits the unshipping of the gaff and sail from the mast while that is stepped, I modelled and had a brass gear made in this shape—

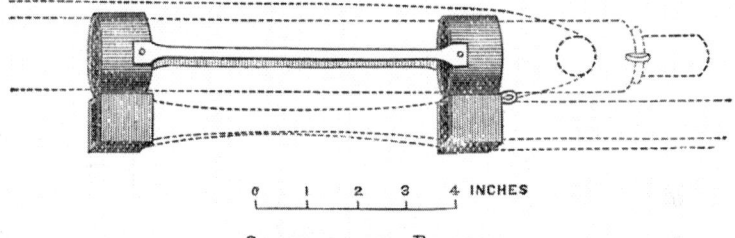

SLIDING-GUNTER BRASS.

It answers perfectly: the gaff can be unshipped from the squares (with the sail laced to it) and the boom untoggled; the sail boom and gaff can then be stowed below, leaving on the mast the brass, into which the dandy can be shipped and used as a tri-sail, which, when fishing or shooting, is quite large enough, and has no boom swinging about.

By lacing the sail to the boom, a much smaller spar can be carried than would be required when a lacing is not used.

Reefing this sail is performed in the same way as in the standing lug for the first reef, but the second reef is more snug: the tack of this reef is at the heel of the gaff, which, when down, only requires the cringle on the after leach to be hooked, tie points, and the reef is in. The sail can be brailed up by a double topping lift from the mast-head, the gaff may be up, or, when snugness is required, it should be down.

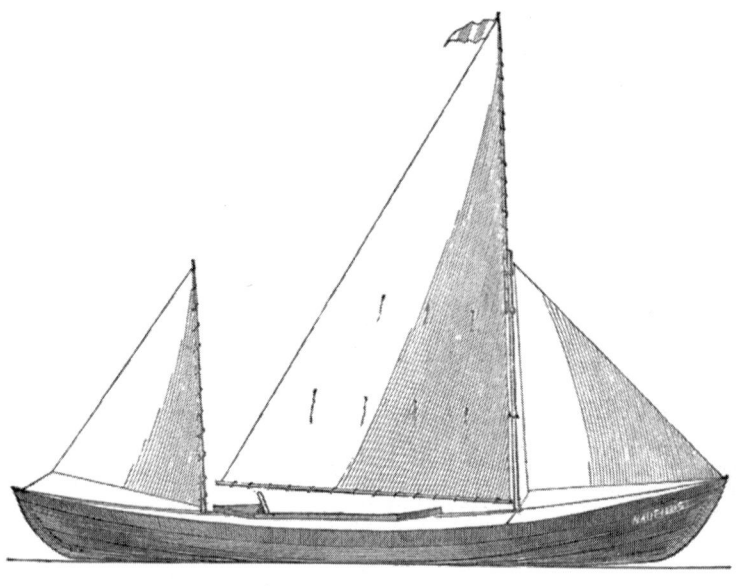

Sliding-Gunter Rig.

One of the most dangerous manœuvres in sailing a canoe is "jybing" when running before a stiff breeze and short breaking sea; for this operation the sliding-gunter "cuts out" all other rigs: the great advantage is the pointed peak being "up-and-down" amidships; for jybing the boom is topped up, spilling the sail, and then dropped on the other tack, during which time the canoe, not receiving any sudden pressure of wind on either side, maintains her course. But in a gaff or yard headed sail, the wind takes the head of the sail and carries it across with a sudden "flop," causing the boat to "come up in the wind," when, if not successfully prevented by letting go the sheet and putting the helm "hard up," the following sea will catch her abaft the weather-beam and break over her amidships. At such a juncture the halliards should not be let go, as the sail being at right angles to the boat, would all fall overboard and render her still more unmanageable.

No *after sail* should ever be carried when running in fresh breezes.

The paddle should always be shifted to the coming leeside before the sail is changed to that side, in anticipation of "broaching to."

The sliding spreet.—Before passing from *sails and rigs* to *fittings*, it may be of some use to give a short description of a "cross bred" rig I have been planning. By various trials with different rigs I found that the *spreet sail stood best* and that the *sliding gunter* was the *handiest*.

I was desirous of obtaining the good qualities of both in one rig, losing sight of the high peak of the sliding-gunter and the lofty mast of the spreet-rig.

This was effected in a cross between the spreet-sail and the sliding-gunter, showing a good deal of the sliding-gunter breed.

It is a well-known fact that the high pointed peak of the sliding-gunter is more ornamental and handy than useful, and that a square-headed sail holds the "best wind;" but a square-headed sail, to be large enough, requires a very lofty mast and long spreet, both of which the sliding-spreet is intended to obviate.

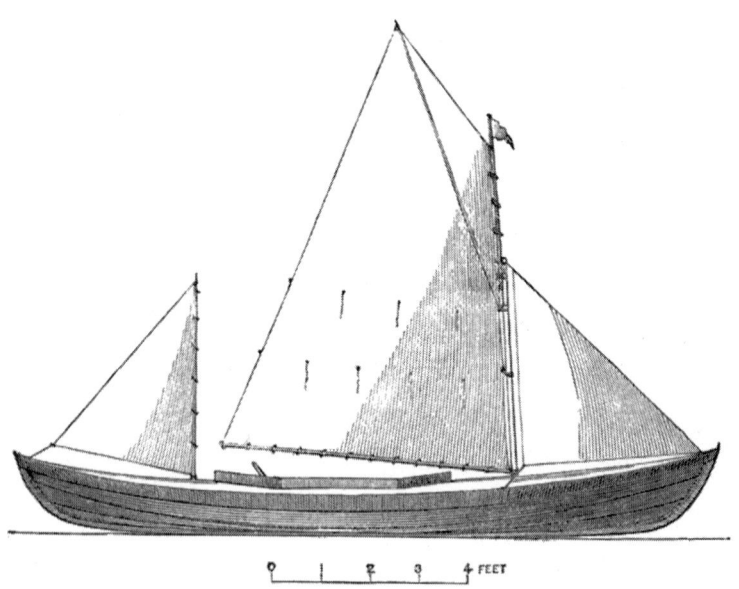

SLIDING-SPREET RIG.

I have fitted and tried this new plan at Weymouth, in various weather and states of sea, and always with the most satisfactory results. It stands well, reefs quickly, and can be lowered, brailed up, unshipped, and stowed below in almost as short a time as it takes to describe the manœuvre.

The rig was tried on a canoe measuring 15 feet length, beam 2 feet 4 inches, depth 1 foot; *mainsail*, luff, 6 feet, of which 3 feet are on the gaff; head 3 feet, leach 9 feet, foot 6 feet, spreet 6 feet from peak to lower part of gunter-brass; two reefs, double topping lift.

Jib.—Luff 6 feet, leach 4 feet, foot 4 feet. The head, luff, and foot of the sliding spreet-sail require roping, the selvage of the stuff being on the leach.

The close-reef tack is at the heel of the gaff, and the cringle on the after-leach hooks on to a hook on the boom.

The first reef, tack hooks to cringle on the fore-end of the boom.

The spreet ships into a short "snotter" made fast to the gunter-brass.

On lowering the gaff a mast of only half the former height is obtained; this is very handy, both in river and sea work, passing under bridges, ships' warps, and boarding vessels.

It makes an invaluable *bad weather* rig, as, when close-reefed, one can still unship the spreet, thus forming a small three-cornered sail, very handy in the sudden sharp squalls one meets with in Egypt and on the Mediterranean coast of France.

Spars.—Sliding-spreet mast, deck to head, 4 feet 3

inches; boom, 6 feet; spreet, 6 feet; gaff, 4 feet; dandy-mast, deck to head, 4 feet 6 inches.

Dandy.—In rigging a canoe the great object is to keep the body of the sails low, to have them so placed as to balance the pressure of wind, and also to be able to lessen the pressure on any part, according as may become requisite by shift of course or wind.

Looking at the canoe in her relative proportions to other boats, her length is out of all proportion to her beam and depth, for sailing purposes; therefore, whether eighteen, sixteen, or fourteen feet long, she must still be regarded as a specially long, narrow, and shallow boat, thus requiring low-bodied sails, so placed as to receive the pressure of the wind on each sail, in the requisite proportion for her clean and straight progress through the water.

A boat, when her sails are properly balanced, ought, when "close-hauled," to require only "a small weather helm." A canoe rigged with a lug and foresail only, usually requires constant "keeping to the wind," therefore, if a small mizen or dandy is added, it keeps her to the wind, and abolishes the drag-water of "lee helm." The requisite size of the dandy will be easily ascertained by the helm she carries; if the dandy is too far aft, or too large, she will carry "large weather helm," in which case, it must be reduced till the helm can be carried nearly amidships.

The advantage of a *dandy* rig over a *yawl* is that the dandy, being jib-headed, can be simply rolled round the mast until the correct balance is obtained; whereas the mizen, having a square head with a yard on it, must be reefed. The amount of dandy-sail used requires altering according to the size of the foresail and amount of mainsail set; therefore, to have the sail bent to a revolving mast, and her clew hauled aft by an outhaul, will be found the most convenient plan. When running, it should be taken in, as after-sail takes the wind from the others, when the wind is right aft, and causes her to yaw about and steer badly.

The Foresail may be fitted in many ways, but the way I have found to be the most convenient is—a loop at the head, a loop at the tack, and a double sheet; place the head loop over the mast-head, by means of the boat-hook, bend the painter, which is rove through the stem, on to the tack-loop, and haul out, keeping one sheet on each side of the mast; in this way it can be set and taken in from one's seat.

Foresails are seldom useful when travelling, except on a long "board," with a beam wind; and even then, should one be capsized by a sudden squall, the foresail is the sail most likely to hinder one's efforts in unshipping the mast to allow the canoe to right herself. For racing and fancy cruising in fine weather foresails are a *sine quâ non*.

CHAPTER XXVII.

FITTINGS — PADDLES — STEERING — RUDDERS — CAMPING OUT — LEEBOARDS — CENTREBOARDS — OUTRIGGERS — SIDEBOARDS — WHEELS — CLEATS — PUMPS — BALLAST — SAILMAKING AND RIGGING — HATCHES AND APRONS.

Paddles.—For sailing and home work, a 7 foot paddle is quite long enough; but on a cruise, where the paddle is used sometimes during several consecutive hours, also for shoving, punting, and steering, an 8-foot paddle has the advantage. The difference in weight is quite insignificant, but the extra length gives it a far better hold in the water. The extra length also lessens the amount of drippings on deck by their falling over instead of inboard.

The dimensions of the handiest paddle for a variety of work are—length, 8 feet; depth of blade, 7 inches; length of blade, 1 foot 6 inches; circumference of shaft, 4 inches. It should be made of yellow pine, without knots, and a good plan for stowage is to have it jointed at the middle by means of ferrules: a paddle fitted thus can be used as a feathering paddle—that is, the edge of the blades can be turned at right angles to one another; but unless you always use it in that style and are accustomed to it, at the most critical moment, making a back stroke to avoid "broaching to" when running before a heavy sea, if you make a false stroke by dipping the paddle into the water, with the blade "fore and aft," a swamp is certain. For travelling, the paddle should be flat and rounded at the ends, with a strip of copper to prevent splitting the blade when roughly used amongst rocks.

An india-rubber ring just outside the hand on each side will arrest the drippings, and cause them to drop outboard.

Spoon-bladed paddles hold the water best, but are more tiring and much weaker than flat blades; also they are no use in steering when sailing.

Steering.—There are three ways of steering when sailing, either with the paddle under the arm, the paddle in a crutch at the side, or with a rudder. The first is a very inconvenient mode, as one hand is always required for the paddle, and when reefing, the paddle must be laid across the knees, in which position it is greatly in the way, also very liable to be knocked overboard. Steering with the paddle in a small crutch at the side of the canoe is, I think, the easiest and handiest of all steering gear. The paddle rests in a crutch, and a slight shove either out or inboard is sufficient to steer in light winds; in a strong breeze the hand is required. In running before a heavy sea the paddle is the only safe steering gear, as the boat is apt to "lose her way" in the trough, when a rudder would have no power, but a stroke on the quarter with the paddle keeps her "end on." All whale-boats and most life-boats steer with an oar when running.

The Massulah boats of Madras are always steered by one, and sometimes two, oars on the quarters; they put off, board ships, and beach again, during a heavy sea and surf. Their peculiar build has a good deal to do with their surviving the bumps received in beaching. Instead of nailing the planks to one another, as in English boat-building, layers of cotton and jute are placed between the planks, which are then sewn together by cocoanut fibres. Built in this way, the boat is able to "work" without breaking up. This mode of building only defends them from being smashed on the beach; it is the skill of the steersman which gets the boat safely over the heavy seas and through the roaring surf. This is always done by steering with oars, not rudders. Most of these boats "leak like a sieve," so they are generally half filled with brushwood, on which the cargo is placed to prevent its getting wet. They are the most lubberly-looking sea-boats I have ever seen.

The rudder can be shaped and fitted in many

RUDDERS AND GEAR.

different ways. To the curved stern-post it may follow round (Fig. 1), but this has two glaring disadvantages—first, it becomes a "dragwater" when in any other direction than fore and aft; secondly, it is liable to become a "dragweed" when the lower part protrudes to port or starboard, accordingly as the tiller is port or starboard. To avoid these faults, some rudders are formed with the curve aft (2), but a good deal of steerage-power is lost by the open space between the lower part of the stern-post and the rudder.

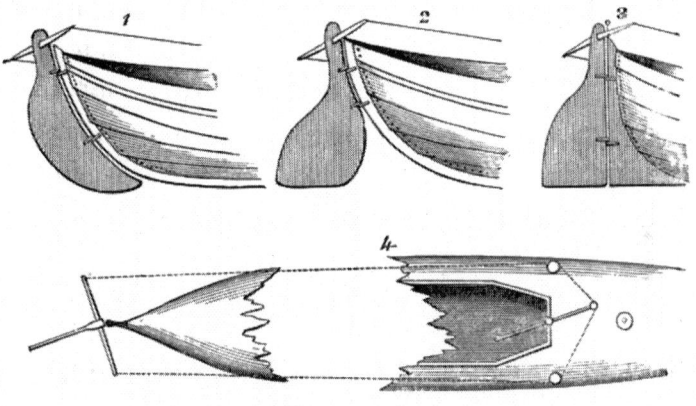

RUDDERS AND GEAR.

The most effective style is with a straight stern-post (3). This does very well for a canoe which is only used on large lakes or the sea, but in travelling, the square stern-post would be awkward in beaching and quick turning. All rudders are in the way when anything falls overboard. "Backing astern" being then suddenly needed, the rudder naturally inclines to one side or the other, retarding the efforts to regain the floating (or sinking) object.

Rudders may be fitted with the ordinary "pintle and gudgeons;" or, in the case of the straight stern-post, with a long pin passing through gudgeons both on rudder and stern-post. There are two ways of working the rudder—either with a whole yoke and yoke-lines, or a half yoke with boat-hook hooked on. The "yoke-lines" should lead along the deck both sides, passing through two small blocks (*hooked* on to the jib-sheet eye-bolts), and ends fast to a tiller working on its centre, as a pivot, on the forward combing, or foremost end of the hatch. When fitted in this way, the canoe can be steered by pressing the knees on either side of the tiller.

Camping out.—Though the sails can cover the hatch at night when the sleeping berth is required, it is far better when on a long cruise, in which various weather is encountered, to have a mackintosh sheet with which to form a tent, and it will be found to stow away in a very small space. By lashing the paddle from mast to mast at 1 foot 6 inches from the deck, then spreading the mackintosh sheet about 8 feet long by 4 feet 6 inches broad over it, and lacing the ends round the masts and sides to the deck cleats, a rain and wind proof cabin is formed; a slit halfway up one (the lee) side, acts as a convenient doorway by which to enter without disturbing the rest of the fabrication; cooking, reading, and writing, can all be comfortably accomplished inside.

But the most important item is first to make a perfect bed for the canoe to rest on ; if this has been neglected, strained timbers and a leaky boat are the consequence.

The certitude of having good cabin accommodation always ready on board, relieves one of that anxiety which too often destroys the calm and ease of the most enjoyable part of the twenty-four hours (the cool of the evening), with gloomy questioning thoughts as to whether one may find any place to put up at for the night.

Leeboards.—A canoe of itself has not enough keel nor depth to prevent her drifting to leeward when sailing "on a wind," therefore many dodges have been tried to give her the requisite lateral resistance, such as "sliding, drop, or centre keels," the deep keeled outriggers (used by the sailing canoeists of Madras, Ceylon, &c.) and leeboards of various shapes.

The *Centreboard* requires a "well case," which is very cumbersome, at the bottom of the boat; it at once puts sleeping in her out of the question; the slit required for the keel weakens the boat considerably amidships, even though it were cut in the garboard streak, and after a bump or two she is sure to leak: a plan was suggested some time ago for fitting canoes with the centreboard in a mackintosh bag, so that when the keel was up it could be folded flat on her floor. But on this principle the bag would still remain full of water, and when the keel was let down whence could it derive support against the strain caused by its lateral resistance?

The sailing *outrigged* canoes of the Bay of Bengal are not such weatherly craft as some people imagine them to be. The chief benefit they derive from their outrigger is, stability under a press of sail; it has very little to do with their weatherly quality, as it is carried to *windward*, and in strong breezes is only slightly immersed; if it were carried to leeward it would help more in keeping the canoe from drifting, but at the same time, when pressed by strong breezes it would tend to "stop her way," and from the great space it occupies would never do for the cruising canoes, which are now under consideration.

Leeboards.—For ordinary pleasure cruising, the trouble of using a leeboard is hardly repaid by the very small amount of "weather gauge" gained on short tacks; but on a long voyage where time and strength must be economized, many a side slant of wind may be successfully sailed to by the help of a well-proportioned and fitted leeboard.

I have tried many different kinds and with various

results: some required too much trouble and tinkering in fitting on, and after all, broke down and refused duty; others flushed the water, not being placed exactly fore and aft; the fore end should be slightly inclined inboard from the parallel of her fore and aft line. The one I now always use is very simple both in make and fitting. It consists of a flat piece of deal with a small beading of oak placed on

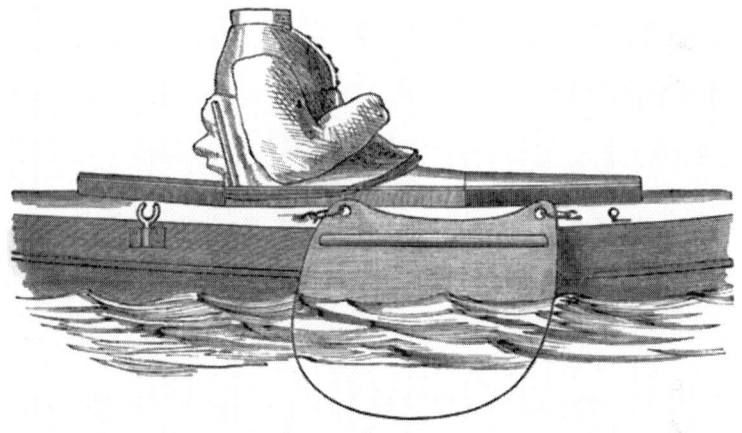

LEE-BOARD.

either side across the grain at its top. These beadings should be covered with leather to avoid chafe as they rest against the topstreak. At each upper corner are holes, into which grummets are spliced; these grummets are dropped over the lee cleats (before halliards, &c. are made fast), the board is dropped over the side and a perfect leeboard is rigged, and can be taken in in a moment.

Another good method is to have a *side-board* fixed on *one side*, working in centre-board fashion, by means of a band of brass, copper, or zinc, which passes outside it, and screwed to the topstreak at each end. The apex of the board is fixed by a pin through this sheet of metal into the topstreak, and the after end can be lifted or lowered and pinned as required in the same manner.

This mode saves the trouble of shifting it over when going on the other tack, but at the same time is likely to strain the topstreak.

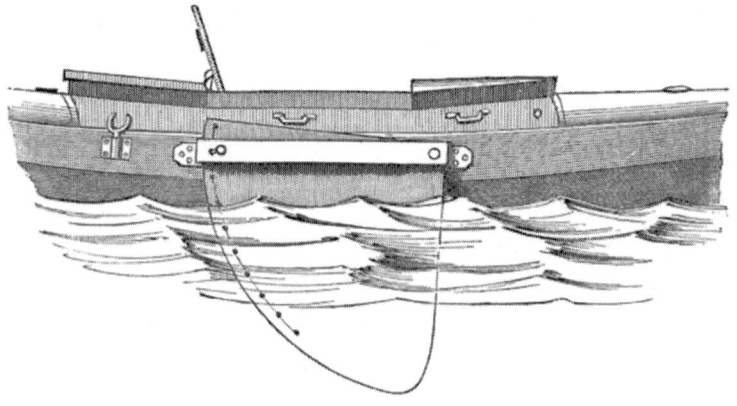

SIDE-BOARD.

Lee-boards have to stand a very great strain, therefore the grain of the wood should point "up and down," and all fastenings should be securely made. I have carried away strong woven cord grummets in fair "cracking on;" and at

Marseilles, last winter, in a N.W. gale, when close hauled under two reefs in smooth water inside the outer breakwater, my lee-board wrenched the foremost cleat nearly out of the deck; the moral of which is, have the cleats screwed through the deck into a beam or knee, which had not been done in the case of the aforesaid cleats.

Canoe Wheels.—Many a strained back and aching muscle, caused by having to drag or carry the canoe over weirs, locks, and up to houses, when no man came in sight to aid, and many a sixpence or shilling when they did aid, would have been saved, in my Swedish cruise, by a small pair of wheels; their stowage space and weight is a mere nothing—a pound or two: one's own body might be that much heavier after dinner, and the difference hardly perceptible.

Not that I mean to go without my dinner to carry the wheels: I intend having both. The wheels don't add to her weight when land transporting, as they are on the ground under the boat, and when afloat they are ballast, and in a leaky boat make first-rate " dunnage," on which to stow "dry goods."

There are many ways of fitting canoe wheels ; but the two chief points for consideration are, to work well when rigged and to stow well when unrigged.

The best forms I know of are shown in this sketch :—

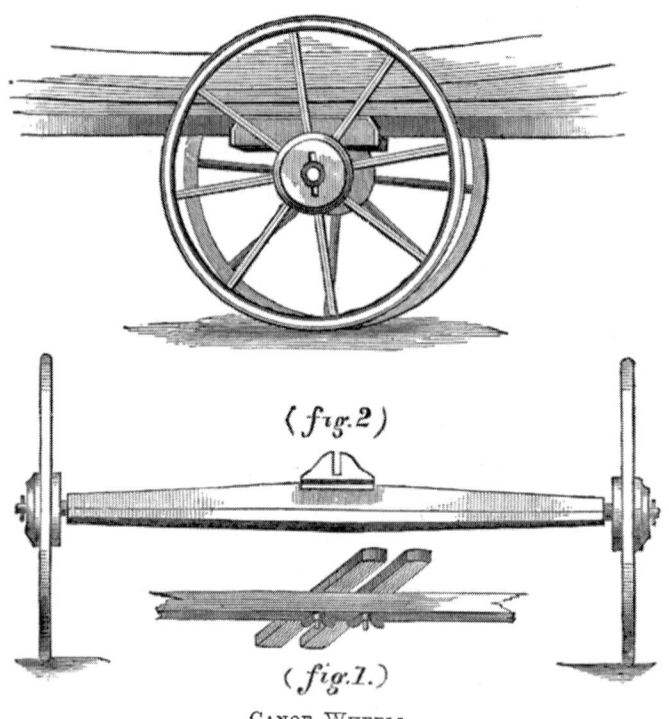

CANOE WHEELS.

In both these styles the wheels are the same, *i.e.* well-made spoke wheels, 1 foot in diameter, and ¾ of an inch thick. Fig. 1 is the way I had mine fitted last summer; a square iron axletree, ¼ an inch wide each side, and 2 feet 6 inches long, with two holes, each 1½ inches from the centre; on the upper side two pieces of wood are placed at right angles to the axletree and parallel to each other, far enough apart for the keel of the canoe to fit neatly in; a long screw from each of these pieces passes through the holes in the axletree, by which screws they are firmly fixed with thumb-nuts. The wheels fit on in the ordinary way, with "washer and lynch-pin" (see Fig. 2),—the plan of L. Young, Esq., C.C. The axletree is of wood, and the groove-piece of wood firmly bolted on; to the ends of the axletree are screwed iron bolts, on which the wheels travel.

Cleats.—The best, in my opinion, for all work and all weather, are the ordinary copper deck cleats.

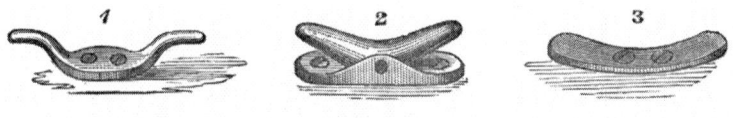

CLEATS.

If the canoe is heavily rigged they must be large and strong, especially the halliard cleat. Before screwing them to the deck a piece of mackintosh should be placed between the cleat and the deck: this allows the cleat a *little* play, thus easing the sudden jerks, which otherwise loosen the screws. Fig. 2 is a patent cleat, the property of which is, that each extra turn of line taken jams the first tighter, and that, when in a hurry, one round turn will hold "till all's blue."

Fig. 3 was shown to me by Mr. Macgregor; it is a thick piece of leather, cut in an oblong form and simply screwed to the deck by two screws; this is very handy for jib sheets and dandy outhaul, but is not strong enough for halliards, lee-board, or topping-lift.

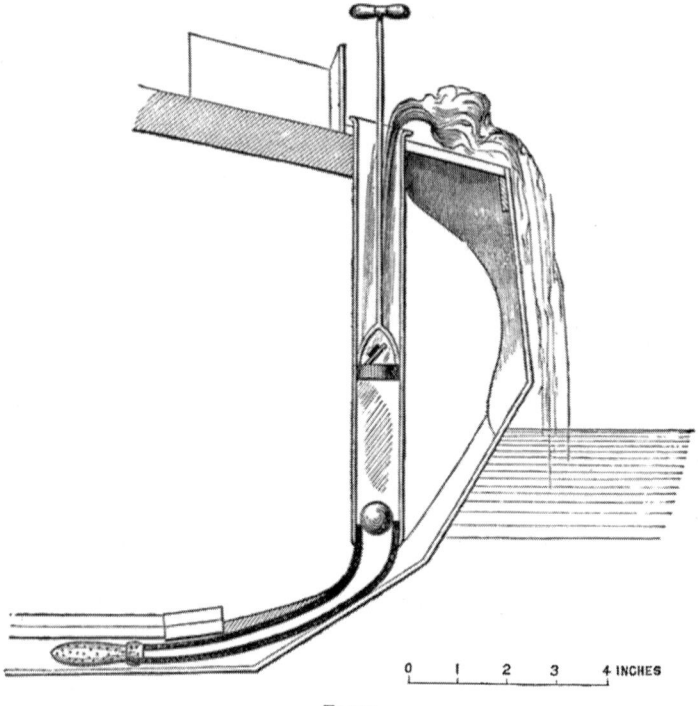

PUMP.

Pumps.—A well-fitted pump would be a great comfort when on a trip some miles from land during bad weather. I have had several times to heave to most carefully in a heavy sea, and to waste time and drift to leeward, whilst baling out the water, which gets in round the mast and from behind one. In some boats it leaks in all round, and if allowed to increase would wet the stores and one's seat.

The best style of pump would be a common hand-pump, either metal or gutta-percha. A cylinder of 1 inch diameter and eight inches depth should be let into the deck close to the combing and alongside a knee and timber; this will reach from the deck to the floor-boards. Into the lower end of this cylinder a tube of smaller diameter must be carefully fitted and fixed ; the lower end of this should be flattened and covered with wire-gauze (to prevent dirt choking it). A round marble or bullet, larger than the diameter of the lower tube, is dropped into the large cylinder, to act as a valve at the bottom ; then the piston-handle or rod, 10 inches long, is added, the lower end fitting the cylinder, and containing a valve, which closes during the up-stroke and opens on the downward, thus bringing with it at each up-stroke nearly as much water as the cylinder holds.

Ballast.—No sailing boat or yacht is complete, nor will she sail well, without ballast. In yachts and large sailing boats the ballast is usually of lead and iron, but in small boats and canoes it should be "water;" then, if she gets capsized, she will not sink, as the water ballast becomes, or is, of equal weight with the water, into which it is thrown, whereas lead or iron remaining the same weight under as above water, sinks her at once, leaving the crew floating about amongst oars and empty bottles, hoping some ancient mariner may come and pick them up.

In the *Nautilus* I carry two tin "oil-cans," capable of containing 1½ gallons each. For a cruise, one can be filled with methylated spirits for the cuisine lamp (only used when no wood is procurable), and the other filled with water when required as ballast, or, as a stock of fresh water when cruising on the briny ocean; all ballast and stores should be lashed to her bottom,—then, if capsized, they help to right her at once.

Sail-making and Rigging.—The size and strength of the sails is usually regulated by the owner's fancy. On the Thames, canoes are constantly seen rigged with sails thick and strong enough, though too small, for large boats; and with others, the very reverse, like pocket-handkerchiefs. I have never seen one "over-masted," or with too much spread of sail, as is so commonly the case with small yachts. Many men say that, "for travelling, sails are useless, and not worth the trouble of carrying." This may be so for trout streams and very tortuous rivers; but when some hundreds of miles of the journey lie in lakes, canals, rivers and seas, a fair wind, or even a side slant, fully repays any little inconvenience sustained by the carriage of the spars and sails when on brook, or against a head-wind.

The material best adapted to canoe sails is fine bleached calico, which can be obtained 6 feet wide; this is a great recommendation, as it avoids the necessity of

SAIL-MAKING.

more than one cloth in the sail. A mainmast of the foregoing dimensions requires the piece of stuff to be 9 feet 6 inches long, by 6 feet wide; this should be spread out flat on a floor, and the four corners nailed down; then the shape of the required sail should be measured, the leach being on the salvage side, and marked by double lines; the inner for the size of the sail, and outer for cutting and turning in: this done, stitch a well-stretched tape half an inch inside the inner line, firmly round the bias edges, to prevent the chance of stretching them when cutting or sewing; this should be left on till the sail is complete.

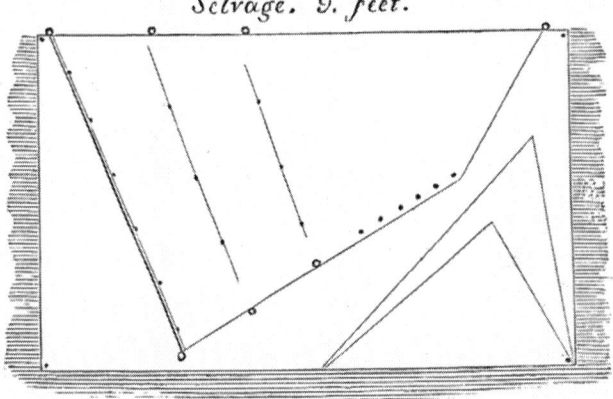

SAIL-CUTTING.

The diagram, scale ¼ inch to 1 foot, shows the method of lining; the triangles represent dandy and foresail, either of which can be made from that piece. I prefer the dandy, as that should be stouter stuff than the foresail, which, is only used for fancy work, and should be of lighter material.

The best roping for canoe sails is small white woven cord; it is easily sewn on, and never shrinks. The lug sail requires strong roping on the luff, and light on the head and foot. The sliding-gunter, light roping on luff and foot. Sliding spreet sail, light roping on head, luff and foot. All sewing should be with well-waxed carpet, or shoemaker's thread. The reef thimbles are worked on with small seizing line: the reef points should be small woven cord, passed through eyelet holes, an overhand knot on each side of the sail, and the ends well whipped with waxed silk: eyelet holes six inches apart on gaff-luff and foot (for lacing); the after-reef cringles should be loops of woven cord, stitched strongly on to the selvage leach.

The dandy requires roping on luff and foot, eyelet holes on luff for lacing, and a clue cringle. The foresail should be strongly roped on the luff, and lightly on the foot; the leaches of both these sails being selvage require no roping. A cane may be fitted as a boom on the foot of the foresail, and with a small hook on the stemhead, will do away with the out-haul, as it can then be hooked on by hand.

A simple and efficient plan of connecting the boom and mast is, tack fast to boom, a brass-headed nail hammered into the boom till only a quarter of an inch projects; this fits into a loop of cord or piece of leather, with a slit in it seized on to the mast, and holds button and button-hole fashion; in this way it can be easily unslipped by handling the boom; or two loops, one on the boom and one on the mast, may be passed through one another and toggled by a small chock of wood (with a lanyard).

Two boxwood blocks, one for the halliards and the other for the toppinglift, should be lashed, one on each side of the mast; cheek sheaves might be let into the mast instead: they would look neater, but the pins holding them would weaken the mast.

All the "strings" should be well-tested woven cord.

Hatches and Aprons.—The covering to my hatchway has undergone many changes. It commenced with the "Rob Roy" mackintosh apron, held up by wooden sides and down to the deck forward by a small cord. This was good for light work, but a heavy slop of sea more than once knocked it in, and water breaking over aft, found no barrier to divert its seaward course. The plan was succeeded by a tin hatch, which was found to be a vast improvement, indeed, with only one drawback—that of sinking, to a certainty, if it fell overboard. Next came a wooden hatch, which, not being properly understood nor fitted, was cast off as a failure; and followed by a half hatch and short apron: this was used chiefly in the Mediterranean and at Southsea. But even this was not quite the thing when running with "a sea on," or in heavy rain. Therefore the wooden hatch has been again called into requisition, and is now so adapted as to be a success. To exclude the water which comes in round the body from rain, or seas, a mackintosh coat is required, with a mackintosh flounce fitted on in a waterproof manner under the arms; the bottom of this flounce has an elastic cord rove in the hem, and is to be placed round outside the hatch-combing, the hatchway-combing, and abaft the back-board, thus forming a sort of tent, of which the captain's body is the tent-pole, as shown in the sketch of the leeboard (page 147). The rest of the coat is left long for walking in rain, and if to be worn in a town, the coat can be turned inside out. It should only have three buttons on front at the breast, and be put on over the head instead of open down the front. The flounce, thus forming a cape round below the arms, must be full behind, to allow of stooping forward, and yet at the same time not deranging its hold on the combing.

If the hatch is well fitted to the combing, when chock home it will exclude any water that breaks over the deck. Should any interstices be discovered, a piece of small india-rubber tubing fast to the combing, upon which the hatch jams, when home, will be found to remedy the defect. A string or piece of elastic should cross over the fore-end of the hatch, and be made fast on both sides to the deck. This prevents the hatch from being lifted by seas, and acts as if a hinge, in the event of a sudden jump out.

CHAPTER XXVIII.

NAVIGATION — CHARTS — COMPASS — BEARINGS — SOUNDINGS — VARIATION OF COMPASS — CURRENTS — LEEWAY — INSTRUMENTS.

CRUISING on lakes whose surfaces cover some hundreds of miles, crossing belts or fiords, and coasting on the sea, require a good chart and compass; also the knowledge of "rule of thumb" navigation, by which to work them.

Charts.—There are two kinds of charts, viz., "General," those which include a large expanse of coast, and give but few particulars; and "Coasting," which give all details necessary for navigation.

On some coasting charts, plans of the various ports are given on a larger scale; all give the various currents, soundings, lighthouses, buoys, rocks, and reefs, and have the true bearings marked on them—an invaluable item in connection with the navigating department.

So long as a river, lake, or sea, is navigable, one is almost sure to be able to obtain a chart of it from marine-store shops or pilots on the spot, though shops in the capitals may deny the existence of any such charts.

Sometimes vessels navigating in the neighbourhood may have important charts, which cannot be spared. In such a case, a sheet of tracing-paper may enable the navigator to obtain all he wants from them in a few minutes.

Most charts may be obtained from J. D. Potter, Admiralty Agent, 31, Poultry. Charts drawn on Mercator's projection are used chiefly for long voyages, but the area of an ordinary canoe cruise will generally be comprehended in a "small scale" coasting chart.

Having the rumblines of the *chart-compass* extended to and in some cases across, the land, saves a great deal of troublesome parallel ruler work when afloat.

The Compass.—The principle and use of all compasses is the same, but they vary very much in appearance.

A ship's compass is lighted at night by a fixed "binnacle lamp," but that of a canoe has to be glared at through the darkness, except in open smooth water, where a lamp can be used.

A *compass course* is the surest guide on lakes or seas when the earth has placed herself between us and the sun. Then the apparent distance and outline of land are very misleading. Much valuable time is wasted, and many a bump on unseen rocks is caused, by dodging about round headlands and islands, trying to ascertain by their true shapes "where we are." *

The clearest diagram I have yet seen for a compass-card is that of the "Rob Roy."

The question of colour has also to be considered—whether *white ground* and *black figures*, as in that card, or *black ground* and *white figures*, are the most distinct.

I have tried both, and think the latter the easiest to decipher in semi-darkness.

COMPASS CARDS.

In purchasing a compass, depth of box, and its relative diameter to the card, should be considered, as freedom in swinging is of vital importance.

I find a compass for ordinary cruising work, slung with a metal cup, more useful than one hanging on mineral, the

* Described in "Rob Roy" on the Jordan.

latter being "too lively" when handled in taking bearings. For cruising work *gimbles* are unnecessary.

The handiest *lubber's point*, both for steering by, and guiding the eye in taking bearings, is a piece of black thread gummed in a straight line *under* the glass and crossing the centre: it is placed under the glass to prevent the gum being melted by rain or spray, which would be the case if it were exposed on the upper surface.

Bearings.—When coasting, the best way to find the canoe's position on the chart, is by the *cross-bearings* of two known fixed objects: draw the lines of these bearings on the chart and their point of intersection is the canoe's position, from which a fresh course can be steered.

Thus, for example, in the Baltic Sea,—after running up outside of the numerous little islands, rocks, and shoals, suppose that it is desired to reach a town which lies out of sight behind these islands; by finding the exact position of the canoe on the chart and then steering as direct a course as intervening islands, &c. will permit, much time and hard climbing of rocks to choose the course by guess-work, will be saved. Let us suppose, in the foreground are small islands and rocks, "as thick as bees," behind them stretches the low, fir-clad mainland, and away to the rear of all, looking blue in the distance, rises the peak of a mountain, whilst on one of the low islands stands a light-house or land-mark.

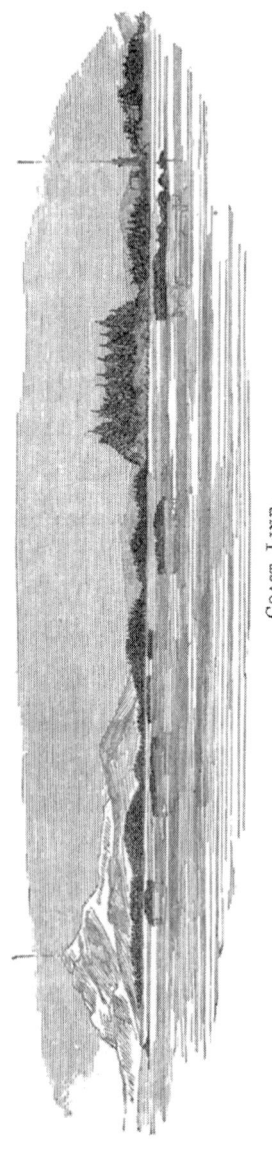

Coast Line.

Take the bearings of the mountain and of the land-mark, correct them for *variation of compass*, draw the lines on the chart, and where they intersect is the position of the canoe; from which shape a course for the town.

Soundings.—As charts give the various depths of water, occasional soundings, taken with a fishing "running line" and bullet, which may be measured on the forward end of the hatchway combing, as it is one foot broad, will help in checking any error in the bearings.

Variation of the compass.—All bearings should be corrected from "compass" to "true" by applying the *variation of the compass*. The amount of variation required (which alters in different parts of the world) will be found printed on the chart in degrees. Turn the variation into points and quarter points, then when it is *easterly* the true course or bearing is found by allowing it to the *right* of the compass course or bearing : and when it is *westerly* by applying it to the *left* of the compass course.

When the "true course" is given and the "compass course" required, easterly variation is applied to the *left* and westerly to the *right*.

For instance, if you wish to get from the mainland to a low island, some six miles off, which is not visible above the horizon, suppose that the *true course* on the chart is E. by N., and there is one point and a half westerly variation; the *compass* course to be steered will be one point and a half to the right of E. by N., namely E. half S.

Currents.—Where *tide* or *current* exists, it is most important that the navigator should endeavour to discover its direction and speed : if it crosses the course, make a good allowance by steering in an "up-current" direction, so as to counteract its drifting tendency.

Existing currents are generally marked on the chart, but this may not always be the case; when there is any doubt it is ascertainable by either of the following easy methods.

If the canoe be in shallow water, drop the sounding lead to the bottom, and the direction in which the canoe drifts from the lead is that of the existing current. Or, (with the canoe unmoved by paddle or wind,) get two distant objects one behind the other in a line; then if they remain so, there is *no cross current;* but if the more distant object begins to shew itself one side or other of the nearer one, there *is* a cross current, which is setting you to the right or left of the objects you are facing.

Leeway.—If the course is to be *sailed* and the wind is nearly abeam, an allowance must be made in a weatherly direction to counteract the effects of *leeway*, which is the angle included between the direction of the *fore and aft* line of the vessel and that in which she moves through the water, or her "wake."

Canoes, like all other vessels of light draft, make a great deal of leeway; except when a leeboard is used, as should be the case on a long tack, such as the six-mile one we pictured when considering the compasses.

When sailing on the starboard tack she will drift to the *left* of her proposed course; and if no allowance is made in the course for leeway, before starting, when she has run her six miles (supposing the angle of leeway at $2\frac{1}{2}$ points) she will be between three and four *miles* to the left, that is dead to leeward of the island; which, if it was a low one, would not be seen at all by the captain, sitting so low in his canoe; he would then have either to take a cruise in search of the island or run back to the main land.

A small, plain "mariner's compass," a parallel ruler, a

INSTRUMENTS.

pair of compasses, a sounding line and charts, are all that is required for safe navigation during an ordinary canoe cruise; but if on a long voyage in unknown lakes and seas, where not only the safety and success of the whole trip depends on the navigation, but accurate geographical results are required, the ship's navigation department must be greatly increased. The compass must be a first-rate one, fitted as an "azimuth compass" (a small tripod on which to fix it for those observations of "azimuth" and "amplitude" would be very handy); a pocket sextant and an artificial horizon (for inland work), book of tables, logarithms and formulæ, chronometer watch, pocket aneroid, wet and dry bulb thermometers, marked sounding line and lead with "arming"* hole, are absolutely necessary to obtain reliable results.

* "Arming" *i. e.* grease in the bottom of sounding lead brings up a sample of the bed of the lake, sea, or river.

CHAPTER XXIX.

COOKING AND CLOTHING—STORES OF FOOD—SHIP'S STORES—USEFUL ARTICLES—WOOD FIRES—"ROB ROY" CUISINE—FRESH WATER ON SALT—CANOE WARDROBE—NIGHT-CLOAK—OVERLAND STORES AND TOWN RIGS.

MAN requires to be fed; without the proper amount of well-cooked food, he cannot enjoy invigorating exercise; and as restaurants and dining-rooms are not often to be met with in the wild lake districts, a small amount of provisions and a heating apparatus, by which to cook them, should be carried. The nature of the provisions is easily decided on by the taste of those for whose consumption they are intended: such as tea (less bulk and weight than coffee required, to attain equal results); sugar, salt, pepper, biscuits (reserved for "no bread" occasions); Leibig's essence of beef (used when without fish or eggs); brandy (to purify water when bad), (it generally is so), and to use when no beer or milk is obtainable: brandy can be bought at almost any village, but look out for the quality before taking it. Matches should be wax, and such as will ignite on *any* dry, rough substance, and should be kept in an airtight box. Quinine; Rhu. pills; methylated spirits for the furnace, and oil for the lamp.

The following is a list of the articles which I have found useful and in some cases indispensable. Money (in gold); small change, in the country coin; a "handle tool chest," nails, screws, wire, &c.; a bottle of varnish, lump of putty; two long sheath knives; a towing line; fishing tackle; pistol (breach-loading, with waterproof ammunition), a dark eye-glass, (used when steering with the sun-glare on the water a-head: it is better than spectacles, as it can be dropped from the eye in a moment without requiring the hand to be taken from its duty,) a mackintosh life-belt, and a well-stocked housewife.

The heating department requires especial care, or many a supperless night will be the consequence. Wood fires can be formed with ease when the wood is procurable and the weather dry; but in wet weather and when fuel is scarce, there is nothing more difficult to perform than to try to boil the soup over hissing, sputtering, and steaming damp twigs, having burnt all the available paper and half one's store of matches, and nearly succeeded in committing suicide in the suffocating smoke.

To avoid these natural impediments to the Crusœan

culinary art, we are luckily enabled to avail ourselves, owing to the enlightenment of the age, of the "Rob Roy Cuisine." This little wonder, when it puts the best of its three legs forwards, and when its buoyant spirits fume forth in firy fury, flashing fitfully in furnace fashion, can boil a quart of soup in the short space of five minutes. It can be obtained of Hepburn, 93 Chancery Lane; and I would say to those who have not got one, get one; and to those who have one, but have not yet tried it on a cruise, they will find the following additions to it most useful. Two different things cannot well be cooked at the same time, by the apparatus in its present state, but by the addition of an extra frying pan (made of tin and used as a lid to the saucepan,) boiling and frying can proceed at the same time over a wood fire. When the spirit lamp is being used for the boiling departments (according to the printed instructions), the spirit measure containing lighted spirits, should be used under the frying-pan; but this, if there is the least breath of wind, becomes a troublesome process: the flame is diverted and constantly blown out: also holding the pan over it for any length of time, which must be done if coffee or soup is to be kept hot in the saucepan at the same time, is not so pleasant in fact as it may seem in fiction. Therefore a small piece of wire gauze should be placed around the spirit measure, forming a tube some 6 inches deep by 15 inches circumference, thus shading the flame and acting as a stand for the frying-pan. The whole contrivance stows in a mackintosh bag, and adds very little to the general weight of stores carried: but to know that one's kitchen fire is on board (in a liquid state) is a source of comfort on coming to a wild night's halting-place after dark.

It is needless to remind cruisers that when voyaging on the Baltic, or other salt water, a stock of fresh water should be carried for making soup or coffee. One may be amongst islands many miles from the mainland, which yield no fresh water.

A sufficiency of clothing is perhaps of more vital importance when travelling on the water than when on dry land. The popular idea of a canoe wardrobe consists in limiting oneself to single specimens of only the most indispensable articles; whereas both health and comfort can only be insured by a dry change and plenty of warm night clothing. There is no special necessity to limit oneself in a wild country by a few ounces. On a Continental stream, with shallow rapids and abundance of villages at which to put up, it is well to have the gear and stores as light as possible; whereas in lake and sea cruising, with the inevitable camping-out at night, wet or dry, the extra weight is compensated by the comfort insured, as well as by the advantages of its ballast properties, which auxiliarate the canoe's sailing qualities in a breeze.

I generally carry a complete change of thick flannels (shirts with collars on), woollen socks, lots of handkerchiefs, boots for villages, wading-shoes, felt hat, flannel cap, warm monkey jacket, flannel coat, &c.

For night the most suitable wrap is an Inverness cape, reaching two feet beyond the feet when lying down in it: this bottom portion can be tied over the feet, like the mouth of a sack. When worn for walking, this long skirt can be buttoned up inside to about the height of the knee. At the back of the neck is a hood (a great safeguard in tent draughts), and the crowning point of the whole is that, when snugly wrapped up for the night, an arm can still be used to fasten the tent-door, put out the light, hold a pipe, &c., without untucking all the rest, as one does when rolled up in a railway-rug.

The shore-going clothing, for town wear, and reserve stores, can be conveniently sent forward in a portmanteau, by overland conveyance, on the intended route.

THE END.

London: Printed by SMITH, ELDER AND Co., Old Bailey, E.C.

SELECT LIST OF WORKS
RECENTLY PUBLISHED.

THE RING AND THE BOOK.
By ROBERT BROWNING. 4 vols. Fcap. 8vo. 30s.

⁎ *The Volumes are sold separately, price 7s. 6d. each.*

"We must record at once our conviction, not merely that 'The Ring and the Book' is beyond all parallel the supremest poetical achievement of our time, but that it is the most precious and profound spiritual treasure that England has produced since the days of Shakspeare."—*Athenæum.*

THE POETICAL WORKS OF ROBERT BROWNING.
New Edition in Six Volumes. Fcap. 8vo. 30s.

⁎ *The Volumes are sold separately, price 5s. each.*

"The size is handy, the type clear, the paper good; making a shapely and convenient book for either the fireside or the country lane."—*Athenæum.*

AURORA LEIGH.
By ELIZABETH BARRETT BROWNING. Tenth Edition. Fcap. 8vo. 7s.

THE POETICAL WORKS OF ELIZABETH BARRETT BROWNING.
Eighth Edition. 5 vols. Fcap. 8vo. 30s.

THE DIVINA COMMEDIA OF DANTE.
Translated into English Verse. By JAMES FORD, M.A., Prebendary of Exeter. Crown 8vo. 12s.

"The *terza rima* has been maintained throughout, and the fact that this has been skilfully accomplished is in itself a claim to high praise. Mr. Ford's translation is as much distinguished by its accuracy as by its easy pleasant flow."—*Academy.*

Select List of Works Recently Published—Continued.

THE ESSAYS OF AN OPTIMIST.

By Sir JOHN WILLIAM KAYE, K.C.S.I. Crown 8vo. 6s.

"We most sincerely trust that this book may find its way into many an English household. It cannot fail to instil lessons of manliness."—*Westminster Review.*

"The essays are seven in number:—Holidays, Work, Success, Toleration, Rest, Growing Old, and the Wrong Side of the Stuff—themes on which the author discourses with bright and healthy vigour, good sense and good taste."—*Standard.*

CONVERSATIONS ON WAR AND GENERAL CULTURE.

By the Author of "Friends in Council," &c. Crown 8vo. 6s.

"Mr. Helps has lost none of his power of writing easy and agreeable dialogues. His illustrations are as abundant as ever. His remarks upon men and manners are as subtle, and, at the same time, as kindly as they were when first he began to chronicle the conversations of Milverton and Ellesmere."—*Athenæum.*

JOURNAL OF THE SIEGE OF PARIS.

By the Hon. CAPTAIN BINGHAM. With a Map. Crown 8vo. 10s. 6d.

"We warmly recommend Captain Bingham's diary to those who read for amusement, coupled with information, and we recommend it specially as most happily uniting lucidity to conciseness."—*Saturday Review.*

FRANCE BEFORE EUROPE.

Translated from the French of M. JULES MICHELET. Crown 8vo. 2s. 6d.

LUCIE'S DIARY OF THE SIEGE OF STRASBOURG.

By a YOUNG LADY OF ALSACE. With Frontispiece and Vignette. Small post 8vo. One Shilling.

THOUGHTS ON HEALTH AND SOME OF ITS CONDITIONS.

By JAMES HINTON. Crown 8vo. 6s.

"A book which must be read as a whole, and read attentively . . . It is sure to convey high suggestions to the thoughtful mind, and can claim to demand for the subject of health a finer recognition than that of the mere manual of the apothecary, or the treatise of the dietitian or physiologist."—*Illustrated Times.*

TO SINAI AND SYENE AND BACK IN 1860 AND 1861.

By WILLIAM BEAMONT. Second Edition. Demy 8vo. 7s.

Select List of Works Recently Published—Continued.

THE ANNALS OF RURAL BENGAL.

By W. W. HUNTER, LL.D. Vol. I. "The Ethnical Frontier." Fourth Edition. Demy 8vo. 18s.

"Mr. Hunter, in a word, has applied the philosophic method of writing history to a new field. The grace and ease and steady flow of the writing, almost make us forget, when reading, the surpassing severity and value of the author's labours."—*Fortnightly Review.*

JOURNEYS IN NORTH CHINA, MANCHURIA, AND EASTERN MONGOLIA,
WITH SOME ACCOUNT OF COREA.

By the Rev. ALEXANDER WILLIAMSON, B.A.

"The information is especially voluminous regarding the scientific and practical geology of the country, the latter being especially important from the wonderful stores of coal, iron, and other mineral productions which China contains."—*Economist.*

MODERN RUSSIA;

Comprising:—Russia under Alexander II., Russian Communism, the Greek Orthodox Church and its Sects, the Baltic Provinces of Russia. By Dr. JULIUS ECKARDT. Demy 8vo. 10s. 6d.

"Dr. Eckardt's able work cannot but be read with the deepest interest by every student of politics."—*Standard.*

THE MAGYARS;
THEIR COUNTRY AND ITS INSTITUTIONS.

By ARTHUR J. PATTERSON. With Maps. 2 vols. Crown 8vo. 18s.

"Mr. Patterson's book is a remarkably thorough and valuable one, quite indispensable to any one who desires to understand the social and political phenomena of Eastern Europe."—*Saturday Review.*

ROUND ABOUT PICCADILLY AND PALL MALL;
OR, A RAMBLE FROM THE HAYMARKET TO HYDE PARK.

A Retrospect of the various changes that have occurred in the Court end of London. By HENRY B. WHEATLEY. With Illustrations. 8vo. 16s.

"Every page of this handsome volume is fraught with matter of interest to the historian, the student of social development, the antiquarian, and the *flaneur.*"—*Daily Telegraph.*

HISTORY OF ART.

By Dr. WILHELM LUBKE. Second Edition. 415 Illustrations. 2 vols. Imperial 8vo. 42s.

"Dr. Lubke's book is evidently intended for popular reading and study—popular, we mean, for those of cultivated minds; his critical remarks, moreover, are based on knowledge and discrimination."—*Art Journal.*

Select List of Works Recently Published—Continued.

THE LIFE OF GOETHE.

By GEORGE HENRY LEWES. New Edition. With Portrait. Demy 8vo. 16s.

"One of the best biographies in English or in any other language."—*Saturday Review.*

ARISTOTLE:
A CHAPTER FROM THE HISTORY OF SCIENCE;

Including Analyses of Aristotle's Scientific Writings. By GEORGE HENRY LEWES. Demy 8vo. 15s.

"Mr. Lewes says in his Preface that this monograph represents part of a study of that first period in the history of science, which he hopes to mature into a sketch of what might be called the Embryology of Science. But if he do not live to complete the whole design, here is at any rate a part of it, complete in itself, from which the English reader may learn what even few Greek scholars distinctly know—the character, and worth, and influence of Aristotle's scientific teaching."—*Examiner.*

CULTURE AND ANARCHY:
AN ESSAY IN POLITICAL AND SOCIAL CRITICISM.

By MATTHEW ARNOLD. 8vo. 10s. 6d.

"The book is rich in pieces of thinking, if not as a whole, and although it may be full of errors, and false impressions, and exaggerations . . . We are always coming upon something fresh and bright."—*Spectator.*

ON THE STUDY OF CELTIC LITERATURE.

By MATTHEW ARNOLD. 8vo. 8s. 6d.

"Some of the most exquisite prose lectures in the English language."—*Spectator.*

ST. PAUL AND PROTESTANTISM:
WITH AN ESSAY ON PURITANISM AND THE CHURCH OF ENGLAND.

By MATTHEW ARNOLD. Second Edition. Crown 8vo. 4s. 6d.

"Mr. Arnold deserves our thanks for having in so large a measure drawn out the true ideals of St. Paul from their accidental surroundings, and shown how unlike is his theology to the favourite systems of Puritanism."—*Edinburgh Review.*

FRIENDSHIP'S GARLAND:
BEING THE CONVERSATIONS, LETTERS, AND OPINIONS OF THE LATE ARMINIUS, BARON VON THUNDER-TEN-TRONCKH.

Collected and Edited, with a Dedicatory Letter to Adolescens Leo, Esq., of the *Daily Telegraph*, by MATTHEW ARNOLD. Crown 8vo. 4s. 6d.

"The book is a delightful one to read. Mr. Arnold wields his weapon of satire with rare skill."—*Spectator.*

SMITH, ELDER & CO., 15, WATERLOO PLACE.

Printed in Great Britain by
Amazon.co.uk, Ltd.,
Marston Gate.